The Language of Science and Faith

Karl W. Giberson
Francis S. Collins

Copyright Page from the Original Book

InterVarsity Press
P.O. Box 1400, Downers Grove, IL 60515-1426
World Wide Web: www.ivpress.com
E-mail: email@ivpress.com

InterVarsity Press® is the book-publishing division of InterVarsity Christian Fellowship/USA®, a movement of students and faculty active on campus at hundreds of universities, colleges and schools of nursing in the United States of America, and a member movement of the International Fellowship of Evangelical Students. For information about local and regional activities, write Public Relations Dept., InterVarsity Christian Fellowship/USA, 6400 Schroeder Rd., P.O. Box 7895, Madison, WI 53707-7895, or visit the IVCF website at <www.intervarsity.org>.

Design: Cindy Kiple
Images: DNA strands: mohamed sadath/iStockphoto
flower: Bradley Murray/iStockphoto
earth: alengo/iStockphoto

ISBN 978-0-8308-3829-5

Printed in Canada ∞

InterVarsity Press is committed to protecting the environment and to the responsible use of natural resources. As a member of Green Press Initiative we use recycled paper whenever possible. To learn more about the Green Press Initiative, visit <www.greenpressinitiative.org>.

Library of Congress Cataloging-in-Publication Data

Giberson, Karl
The language of science and faith: straight answers to genuine questions/Karl Giberson, Francis Collins.
p.cm
Includes bibliographical references and indexes.
ISBN 978-0-8308-3829-5 (Hardcover: alk. paper)
1. Religion and science. I. Collins, Francis S. II. Title.
BL240.3.G63 2011
231.7'652—dc22

2010040599

P 16 15 14 13 12 11 10 9 8 7 6 5 4 3 2 1
Y 24 23 22 21 20 19 18 17 16 15 14 13 12 11

This optimized ReadHowYouWant edition contains the complete, unabridged text of the original publisher's edition. Other aspects of the book may vary from the original edition.

Set in 16 pt. Verdana

TABLE OF CONTENTS

Praise for The BioLogos Foundation

"Christians and secularists alike are in danger of treating 'Darwin vs. the Bible' as just another battle-front in the polarized 'culture wars.' This grossly misrepresents both science and faith. BioLogos not only shows that there is an alternative, but actually models it. God's world and God's word go together in a rich, living harmony."

N. T. Wright, author of *The Challenge of Jesus*

"[The BioLogos team] may be the only people in the world capable of pulling off this project. They have courage as well as unquestioned respect from both sides of the debate, which has long begged for bridge-builders."

Philip Yancey, author, editor, *Christianity Today*

"A wise, constructive rapprochement between faith and science is one of the world's urgent needs, and this need will only intensify as the global era raises a host of new ethical issues. Few people have the expertise, wisdom and prestige to make such a contribution. I welcome The BioLogos Foundation warmly."

Os Guinness, EastWest Institute

"Many people today, both secular and Christian, want us to believe that science and religion cannot live together. Not only is this untrue, but we believe that a thoughtful dialogue between science and faith is essential for engaging the hearts and minds of individuals today. The BioLogos Foundation provides an important first step toward that end."

Tim Keller, author of *The Reason for God*

Preface

The world is awash in books about the relationship between science and religion. Why do we need another one?

The short answer is that this conversation is important. Some topics—raising children, looking after the planet, improving society, searching for meaning—merit continuous consideration. No book, no matter how grand, will ever close any of these conversations—for each generation, each decade, even each year, brings its own fresh set of issues and new perspectives.

The intersection of science and religion is an important crossroads, for it is there that the world of facts meets the world of values. It is there that we ask our deepest questions: How did we get here? Does our existence have a purpose? Does God exist? How is God revealed in the world? How do we relate to the rest of nature? It is there that we reflect on our religious commitments and decide what to embrace as ultimate truth.

The Language of Science and Faith surveys this intersection. The authors are evangelical Christians, committed to the historic truths of Christianity and the central role of the Bible in communicating those truths. But as scientists, the authors are mindful that the changing understanding of the natural world invites continuous reconsideration of some of those truths, particularly those relating to the natural world.

Sometimes, as with Galileo, this changing understanding can seem threatening to faith. Other times, as seen recently with the discovery that the laws of nature are fine-tuned for life, this changing understanding is wonderfully faith-affirming.

The intersection of science and religion is a controversial place, filled with potholes, poisonous vines and landmines. Countless assertions, some of them contradictory, are made by Christians with great force on many topics, including the age of the earth, the source of morality, the nature of the Genesis creation account and the origins of humankind. The authors are mindful of these controversies and have striven to offer words of reconciliation and harmony, seeking to avoid adding fuel to fires that have been burning far too long. On the other hand, as scientists, the authors are convinced that there are truths about the natural world that must be confronted, no matter how disturbing they seem. But as Christians, the authors are also convinced that there are certain theological truths—like God is the Creator—that must be integrated into any understanding of nature if it is to be a Christian understanding.

On topics where legitimate disagreement exists, readers are offered a range of possibilities consistent with what is known about the natural world and the Bible. The approach to such controversies presented here derives from the belief that God has provided two distinct, complementary and reliable revelations—the Bible and the natural world. *The Language of Science and Faith* seeks a harmony in which the insights of both are respected and taken seriously, and one is not automatically assumed to trump the other.

This book is organized within a framework of questions. Each chapter gathers a collection of closely related topics and presents them as responses to questions. The authors hope this will make it easy for readers to find what they are looking for without having to hunt for it.

Books take a long time to go from inspiration to execution, and this one is no exception. In the case of this book, one of the authors, Francis Collins, fully completed his contribution in the spring of 2009, including the signing of the book contract with InterVarsity Press. Shortly after signing the contract he was appointed Director of the National Institutes of Health (NIH), the world's largest medical research institution. Consistent with the expectations of such a federal appointment, he did no further work on this project after he assumed the directorship of the NIH.

Readers interested in continuing the conversation in this book are encouraged to visit www.biologos.or g.

Acknowledgments

All books have a history. This one started with Francis Collins's decision to write *The Language of God: A Scientist Presents Evidence for Belief,* which went on to become a bestseller.

The Language of God told the story of how Francis found harmony between his science and his Christian faith. He was a world-class scientist—he had led the Human Genome Project to a successful completion and then went on to become the head of the National Institutes of Health, where he presently works. But he was also a committed believer with a winsome and inspiring testimony. His story moved readers who were wrestling with questions of faith and science, and seeking the place of rest that Collins had found in his own journey.

Letters and emails poured in, asking for wisdom and insight. Readers wanted to dig deeper. Many had questions not addressed in *The Language of God.* Soon Francis was buried in a pile of "Frequently Asked Questions." Addressing these questions individually was simply not possible, but many of them were passionate and came from people with real struggles. Ignoring them was not an option.

Necessity, as they say, is the mother of invention. So Francis began to think of a way to address these concerns. The result was The BioLogos Foundation, which came to life in 2008 and went online at www.biologos.org in the spring of 2009. The FAQ section of the website contains early versions of answers to the many questions that inspired this project. The BioLogos Foundation has grown into a significant project, but it would never have been born if those many thoughtful readers of *The Language of God* had not taken the time to share their struggles with Francis.

The original FAQs were drafted by Monica Slinkard, David Scudder and Syman Stevens. Syman would remain with Bio-Logos as its full-time executive director until he headed off to Oxford University in the fall of 2010 to pursue a doctorate in the philosophy of physics. Francis met Syman, Monica and David through the Trinity Forum Academy, where all three were fellows and where he served as a mentor to David. He remains appreciative to Doug Holladay for introducing him to the Trinity Forum and to these young scholars.

Jacki Waring, Frederica LaLonde and Heather Wax helped edit some of the original FAQs. And the following consultant reviewers offered scholarly input: Denis Alexander, Jeff Schloss, Owen Gingerich, Darrel Falk, Alister McGrath, Ernest Lucas, Ron Numbers and Ted Davis.

The Language of Science and Faith, however, is not just a collection of FAQs from the BioLogos website. The task of turning this raw material into a book fell to me, and I have endeavored to turn a collection of encyclopedia articles into a readable manuscript. Readers, of course, can make their own judgments about that.

Andy Le Peau, my editor at InterVarsity Press, made many helpful comments throughout the production of this book, which greatly improved the final product.

Thanks also to Darrel Falk, president of the BioLogos Foundation, for encouraging and supporting me in my writing, and for years of deep and meaningful friendship. Owen Gingerich read the entire manuscript carefully and made many helpful suggestions.

And lastly, I acknowledge a debt I cannot begin to repay to my mother, Ursula Giberson, who passed away while this book was being written. She is the reason I grew to love words as a child.

Karl Giberson
Hingham, Massachusetts
June 2010

Introduction

In the beginning God created the heavens and the earth.

GENESIS 1:1

Christians believe that God created the world. It is one of the most central beliefs and important parts of our faith, second only to our belief in the divinity of Christ and the importance of his life, teaching, death and resurrection.

Belief in God as Creator is a wonderful affirmation. To look at the world around us and know it was created by the God we worship and who was revealed in Jesus is extraordinary in so many ways. We marvel at the elegant beauty of flowers, the songs of birds and the scampering chipmunk. Sunsets, mountains, waterfalls and alpine lakes express a grandeur our poets struggle to capture. And yet the laughter of toddlers exploring their new and unfamiliar world with such curious delight is also strangely spectacular, especially as we ponder our deep intuition that we must care for those young lives.

Some of these emotions are captured in hymns like "How Great Thou Art":

O Lord my God, when I in awesome wonder,
Consider all the worlds Thy hands have made;

I see the stars, I hear the rolling thunder,
Thy power throughout the universe displayed.

When through the woods, and forest glades I wander,
And hear the birds sing sweetly in the trees.
When I look down, from lofty mountain grandeur
And see the brook, and feel the gentle breeze.[1]

More than two thousand years ago the psalmist expressed similar sentiments:

When I consider your heavens,
the work of your fingers,
the moon and the stars,
which you have set in place,
what are mere mortals that you are mindful of them,
human beings that you care for them? (Psalm 8:3-4 TNIV)

In the past couple of centuries another layer of extraordinary beauty has emerged. Scientists studying God's creation have uncovered the elegant and hidden foundations of our world. We now understand why the sky is blue and why sunsets are red. We know about chlorophyll and how it gathers energy from the sun to empower plant life. We know that stars like the sun shine by using the energy of nuclear fusion—an almost limitless source of power. Our planet is a fascinating yet fragile sphere suspended like a dust mote in the life-giving rays of the sun. It rotates reliably on its axis, giving us day and night, and revolves around the sun, giving us regular seasons.

Figuring out the shape and the motions of the earth were the first great triumphs of mathematical physics—the enterprise that has uncovered the profound and breathtaking rational undercarriage of the world. Off the radar of our immediate sense perceptions, we now understand that the world is made of invisible atoms and that they are composed of electrons, protons and neutrons. The protons and neutrons are composed of quarks, bound together by gluons. And all of these particles dance to elegant mathematical tunes, reliably and faithfully being themselves so that the world that is made of them will be stable and congenial to life.

Those of us who appreciate mathematics find a beauty buried deep within nature rivaling that of the sunset. The created order radiates with layers of beauty from the sunset to the orbit of the electron, from the song of the bird to the laughter of the child. We strain to summon analogies to describe the remarkable world that God created. Perhaps, in some way, we might think of the creation being like the humble onion, with its layers. Each layer of the creation is beautiful in different ways, and as we unpeel it we encounter so many different kinds of grandeur and beauty.

The richest appreciation of creation requires that we ponder how the wonder encountered on the surface of the world relates to the beauty in the hidden patterns of nature, how the laws of physics illuminate the beauty of the sunset, how our understanding of human nature draws us to the laughter of children, how genetics opens up the mystery of life.

Unfortunately, many Christians cannot fully appreciate how science enriches our understanding of God's creation. They have been robbed of this experience by an unfortunate misunderstanding that the scientific picture of the world is not compatible with their belief that God created that world. For various reasons they have come to fear—and even reject—science.

Doesn't Science Challenge Faith?

Many Christians fear science because some loud atheists have argued that scientific explanations have replaced belief in God as Creator. Scientific theories are proposed for the origin of the stars and planets, or the diversity of life, or the physical universe, and these explanations are said to challenge the idea that God created these things. This is simply not true, of course, as we will show in this book.

On the other hand, some Christians advance a related argument that belief in God rules out various well-established scientific claims. They argue with the same passion as the atheists that scientific explanations for origins compete with the belief that God is the Creator and we must therefore choose one or the other. This is also not true.

This tension puts Christians in a difficult spot. If they truly believe they must make a choice, they have to reject much of what science has learned about God's creation. Science has developed fascinating explanations for how stars originated, to take one example, but we cannot accept that insight into God's creative processes if we believe that this explanation competes with the belief that God created the stars.

The good news is that we do not have to make this choice. The atheists are simply wrong that scientific explanations compete with our belief in creation. And those Christians who agree with them, while correct in their insistence that God is the Creator, take their claims too far when they say that believing in creation means rejecting scientific explanations for origins.

In the pages that follow we share this good news. We understand that this claim is challenging and that many significant questions arise from it. But we also believe that Christians should be liberated from this awkward tension between their faith and the scientific understanding of the world.

We call our view BioLogos, a term coined by one of us and presented in the bestselling book *The Language of God.* The term combines two key ideas: *bios,* referring to life and all the remarkable features of the world necessary to sustain life, which is just about everything; and *logos,* referring to the Christian belief that the world is created by and grounded in the rationality of God. *Logos* appears in one of the most important passages in the New Testament, the prologue to the Gospel of John: "In the beginning was the Word (Logos), and the Word was with God, and the Word was God" (John 1:1).

The BioLogos idea is not radically new, but the novelty of the word gives us a chance to talk about something that has long been disturbing to Christians without having to be constantly reminded of a long negative conversation. Most importantly it gives us a chance to talk about evolution.

What Is BioLogos, and How Does It Relate to Other Ideas About Origins?

BioLogos embraces *theism,* the belief in a God who cares for and interacts with creation. Theism is different than *deism,* the belief in a distant, uninvolved creator who is often little more than the sum total of the laws of nature and who is usually not viewed as personal. BioLogos also embraces science as a reliable way to understand the world. We believe science is an enterprise with great integrity, and that scientists are, in general, honest and objective in their work, and trustworthy in their conclusions. In embracing science we accept that the biological theory known as evolution is a reliable explanation for the development of the diversity of life on our planet. When we combine our theism with our acceptance of science, including evolution, we are embracing the concept of *theistic evolution.*

Theistic evolution is the belief that God created life using natural processes, working within the natural order, in harmony with its laws. So, why don't we simply use the term *evolution* to describe our view? We don't use the term, at least not at this point in our discussion, because it is associated with negative ideas, including atheism, and many readers would have a constant uncomfortable feeling while thinking about it. The word *evolution* carries emotional baggage that we are tossing overboard.

BioLogos, we hope, has no negative baggage yet, but we hope it will accumulate some positive associations over time.

In the pages that follow we will also discuss the other major views held by Christians. These include the popular young earth creationism (YEC) promoted by Ken Ham and the Answers in Genesis organization. YEC interprets the Genesis account of creation literally, concluding that God created the world in six twenty-four-hour days, less than ten thousand years ago. Old earth creationism (OEC) also interprets the Genesis account literally, but allows that the time periods are much longer. The "days" of Genesis, for example, can be periods of time or geological epochs. Hugh Ross's organization Reasons to Believe leads the charge on this view. And finally there is the intelligent design movement (ID), which does not make explicit appeals to the Bible but instead highlights complexities in nature that in their view show evidence of the action of an "intelligent agent." This view is promoted by the senior fellows of the Discovery Institute: Stephen Meyer, William Dembski, Michael Behe and others.

In the course of our discussion we will highlight our various agreements and disagreements with these views. The main distinctive of BioLogos is its affirmation of the generally accepted scientific theories about origins, including evolution, properly understood.

If Evolution Is God's Method of Creation, Why Does It Have Such a Bad Reputation?

When Charles Darwin published *The Origin of Species* in 1859, he produced a major shift in scientists' understanding of biology. Darwin proposed a mechanism for the gradual change of species, a phenomenon already widely accepted based on the fossil record. But the mechanism for this gradual change was unknown, and different ideas were circulating. Darwin's book, the full title of which is *On the Origin of Species by Means of Natural Selection,* proposed a simple mechanism for speciation and then presented evidence for this new theory. That mechanism was *natural selection.*

Evolution by natural selection is sometimes called "Darwinism," although modern Darwinism acknowledges the importance of other types of evolutionary selection. Attaching the theory of evolution to Darwin's name seems to imply a cult that slavishly follows the work of a single scientist, but this is certainly not the case. Most working biologists today actually have little interest in Darwin himself, and few have read *The Origin of Species.* In fact, most scientists do not use the label "Darwinism" any longer. The modern theory of evolution has contributions from many scientists over the last 150 years and has become the core of biology.

When Darwin proposed the mechanism of natural selection, he did not understand the details of how a species' naturally selected traits could be inherited by its offspring. But the Belgian monk Gregor Mendel's research in genetics, addressing that very question, was already underway. By breeding pea plants, Mendel discovered how traits are inherited.[2] Although Darwin did not know of Mendel's work, and neither Mendel nor Darwin lived to see genetics integrated with natural selection, the synthesis of these two theories—which now includes the discovery of the chemical nature of the gene and the development of the science of molecular biology—is called "Neo-Darwinism" or "the modern evolutionary synthesis." The theory, however, is often referred to simply as "Darwinism" or, more appropriately and as we shall do sometimes, "evolution." But we must keep in mind that countless advances in our understanding of evolution have occurred since Darwin. Nevertheless, these advances have provided more evidence for the validity of his theory. There has been no scientific discovery since Darwin—not one—which has suggested that evolution is not the best explanation for the origin of species.

Contrary to widespread misunderstanding and confident assertions by the various anti-evolutionists, evolution is a scientific theory that makes no direct statements about religion. It may have religious *implications,* as many have noted, but these require a certain theological or biblical point of view to make sense. Evolution per se makes no specific statements about God. Because of this neutrality evolution numbers among its adherents everyone from agnostics like Michael Ruse to evangelical pastors like Daniel Harrell, formerly of Boston's famous Park Street Church. And neither Ruse nor Harrell finds any reason to believe that evolution is incompatible with Christianity. In fact, both wrote books arguing for this compatibility.[3]

A few assertive observers claim that evolution carries atheistic connotations, a serious public relations problem for the theory among Christians, as you can imagine. And even though Christians usually define their belief as *theistic* evolution, to indicate that it is God's method of creation, the term *evolution* remains controversial. The negative connotations arose in part because Darwin's theory provided a nonsupernatural explanation for the design of highly complex systems. Prior to Darwin, theologians like William Paley used the remarkable design of things like the eye to argue for the existence of a designing God.

Darwin's explanation of nature's design, however, was not an attack on belief in God. Rather it was simply an alternative explanation for a set of observations that had been used, too eagerly as we now see in retrospect, to *prove* the existence of God using the tools of science—a science that many were enthroning as the source of all knowledge. The work of Isaac Newton reveals a helpful analogy showing why Darwin's theory is not hostile to the idea of God.

Newton, as we learned in high school, discovered the law of gravitation, explaining why the planets don't escape from the solar system but rather orbit the sun. In Newton's day, however, nobody could figure out why all of the planets circled the sun in the same direction, in almost the same plane, and with such consistency. Since the science of Newton's era could not explain this, Newton argued that God must be the source of such an elegant mechanical system. This is what is called a "god of the gaps" argument. Newton found a remarkable system in nature that science could not explain, so he inferred God as the explanation.

A century after Newton, advances by scientists like Pierre Simon de Laplace showed that there was no mystery in the structure of the solar system—a more sophisticated understanding of gravity could explain the things that Newton ascribed to God. Laplace's work certainly did not refute the existence of God—it merely dismantled a popular argument that Newton had used, inappropriately, to prove the existence of God. If Newton had not created this god-of-the-gaps argument for the existence of God, there would have been no disappointment when science closed that gap.

Darwin offered biology what Laplace offered physics—a natural explanation for some remarkable phenomena people were explaining by invoking God. Neither of these cases presents an argument *against* the existence of God.

More recently, advocates of creationism, intelligent design and even new atheism have claimed that accepting evolution (at least in some forms) is embracing atheism. They argue that evolution is incompatible with a theistic worldview. This argument is illogical and philosophically preposterous. It would be like a girl inferring that because her mother, and not her father, bought her a bike, her father must not exist.

BioLogos challenges this linkage between evolution and atheism. In many of its presentations it appears simple-minded and theologically shallow. BioLogos is thus not a strictly scientific theory but rather a holistic explanatory scheme promoting the belief that evolution is a correct science, and that it effectively describes the method by which God created the panorama of life forms that makes the earth so interesting.

But What About Social Darwinism? Doesn't Evolution Justify the

Destruction of the Weak by the Strong?

There is another entirely different objection to evolution, namely, that it must be rejected because it preaches a false gospel of "might makes right." Some even blame evolution for the holocaust![4] The application of evolutionary ideas, like survival of the fittest, to social problems is called "social Darwinism." But social Darwinism is an *entirely different* concept from Darwinism (evolution) and not even remotely a part of or even an extension of Darwin's theory.

Social Darwinism inappropriately applies evolutionary concepts to groups of individuals in a social context. It takes Darwin's theory and turns it into a moral mandate for society, as if survival of the fittest is the *morally appropriate* mechanism for social development and not merely a description of how species evolve over time. When taken to an extreme the result is often discrimination against weaker members of society who are considered less fit by those who wield the power. Hitler's persecution of Jews is the most extreme example, but there are others, including some close to home.

Social Darwinism is closely related to *eugenics,* the science of controlled reproduction for the purposes of changing the human race in accordance with some particular vision. The term was coined by Francis Galton, Darwin's cousin, and comes from a Greek word meaning "well born." Galton promoted eugenics in his influential book *Hereditary Genius,* where he outlined his vision for improving humanity. In another volume he described his program as the simple replacement of "Natural Selection by other processes that are more merciful and not less effective."[5] Unfortunately, history proved eugenics to be anything but merciful.

In the early part of the twentieth century the United States, eager to improve the "fitness" of its citizenry, led the way in passing eugenics legislation.[6] By 1917 more than fifteen states had passed compulsory sterilization statutes for members of society perceived as "unfit" in some way. More than half of the states imposed restrictions on the marriage of those with mental defects.[7] And, in a famous and tragic miscarriage of justice, the Supreme Court ruling of *Buck v. Bell* in 1927 sentenced Carrie Buck to sterilization on the grounds that she was "feebleminded" and an "imbecile." Later evidence revealed she was neither.[8]

The sentiment of the social Darwinists is captured in these chilling words of Justice Oliver Wendell Holmes Jr.: "It is better for all the world, if instead of waiting to execute degenerate offspring for crime, or to let them starve for their imbecility, society can prevent those who are manifestly unfit from continuing their kind."[9]

As Holmes's comment illustrates, social Darwinists ascribe almost all human attributes to inheritance, though these actually arise from a complex mix of genetics, environment and free will choices. They assume that if humans have evolved by a process of natural selection (a factual claim about the past), it is appropriate to discriminate against less fit members of society, using artificial selection (a value judgment about the present).

BioLogos, as well as many other viewpoints, rejects the implied morality of social Darwinism. In fact, social Darwinism is based on an elementary ethical fallacy, well known to every student of philosophy. This fallacy is the logical move from "is" to "ought." You cannot inspect the way things *are,* the "is" of the world, and infer how things *should* be, the "ought" of the world. Simple examples illustrate the foolishness of this reasoning. From the observation that children love to eat gigantic quantities of candy, should we infer that this behavior is "right"? Because things fall down, should we insist that nobody is allowed to invent a device to make them fall up? If blonds have more fun, should we put brunettes in jail if they enjoy themselves too much? And, if animals evolve by the strong destroying the weak—a caricature of evolution, by the way—should we then conclude that it is *right* for the strong to destroy the weak?

Appeals to social Darwinism to justify aggressive social programs are nothing more than our unfortunate tendency to rationalize our selfish agendas. Bigots like Hitler persecuted Jews long before Darwin, and Hitler was hardly an enthusiast for a scientific view of the world.

Because Victorian England was beset with social problems, Darwin did occasionally comment on how his theory related to those problems, and some of his remarks, taken out of context, seem to suggest that he supported the social application of his theory. The following quote is an example:

> With savages, the weak in body or mind are soon eliminated; and those that survive commonly exhibit a vigorous state of health. We civilised men, on the other hand, do our utmost to check the process of elimination; we build asylums for the imbecile, the maimed, and the sick; we institute poor-laws; and our medical men exert their utmost skill to save the life of every one to the last moment.... Thus the weak members of civilised societies propagate their kind. No one who has attended to the breeding of domestic animals will doubt that this must be highly injurious to the race of man.... Hardly any one is so ignorant as to allow his worst animals to breed.[10]

Darwin, however, has been studied extensively by scholars and none of them believe he supported the social extension of his ideas. Many authors have pointed out that this quote from Darwin's *The Descent of Man* has been deceptively taken out of context to give a false picture.[11] Another quotation reveals that even though Darwin assumed an evolutionary account for charity and philanthropy, he disavowed social Darwinism.

Darwin's quotation continues, although not in the texts of the anti-evolutionists who quote it, as follows:

> The aid which we feel impelled to give to the helpless is mainly an incidental result of the instinct of sympathy, which was originally acquired as part of the social instincts, but subsequently rendered, in the manner previously indicated, more tender and more widely diffused. Nor could we check our sympathy, if so urged by hard reason, without deterioration in the noblest part of our nature. The surgeon may harden himself whilst performing an operation, for he knows that he is acting for the good of his patient; but if we were intentionally to neglect the weak and helpless, it could only be for a contingent benefit, with a certain and great present evil.[12]

Although Darwin may not have embraced social Darwinism, anti-evolutionists have argued that an acceptance of his science comes hand in hand with a social Darwinist philosophy. The popular example of this idea is the claim, mentioned previously, that Darwin's ideas influenced Hitler. However, as evangelical biologist Jeffrey Schloss points out, from the simple fact that no Darwinist since the time of Hitler has been led to the same ideas, it seems clear that evolution does not inevitably lead to Hitler's philosophy.[13] Furthermore, human history contains a long and sad chronicle of racial prejudice and even exterminations, most of which existed long before Darwin.

Hitler's misapplication of Darwin's ideas is mirrored in his abuse of Christianity, which he also claimed inspired his anti-Semitism.[14]

A 2009 biography of Darwin, by two of his leading scholars, has even argued that Darwin was quite animated by the way his developing theory *undermined* the leading justification for slavery—namely, that the "inferior" races had a separate origin and were not a part of the same superior biological group as white Europeans.[15] Many scientists justifiably take pride in the way that Darwin's theory, as it developed through the twentieth century, has so thoroughly undermined the basis for racism that we can now say confidently that bright lines separating human races are no longer biologically meaningful. The view that there are "inferior" and "superior" subgroups of humans has been as thoroughly refuted by science as has the idea that the earth is in the center of the universe.

Conclusion

This view of origins is optimistic and upbeat. We note that the negative baggage associated with evolution can be tossed overboard without harm to faith. Evolution does not provide an argument for atheism, and it cannot be used to justify mistreatment of the weak. It has no sinister, dark mask to frighten the children. It is, quite simply, a scientific theory with lots of empirical support, as we will show in subsequent chapters. Theologically, evolution is an extraordinary insight into the remarkable character of God's creation. We live in a world where change is the norm—ice ages, volcanoes, asteroid collisions, floods, the new arrival of species and extinction of others. How marvelous that the natural world has built-in mechanisms to adapt to this changing environment!

1

Do I Have to Believe in Evolution?

Now the earth was formless and empty, darkness was over the surface of the deep, and the Spirit of God was hovering over the waters.

GENESIS 1:2

Because BioLogos takes science seriously, respecting both scientists and the scientific process, we take biological evolution seriously. We view science as a gift from God requiring three things: (1) An orderly, reliable and predictable creation with patterns to be discovered, (2) minds capable of a deep level of abstract thought, and (3) a burning curiosity to understand the world around us. If any of those three things are missing, then we cannot have science.

When there is a near-universal consensus among scientists that something is true, we have to take that seriously, even if we don't like the conclusion. We don't have to accept everything blindly, of course, just because scientists believe it, but we should demand compelling reasons for rejecting such a consensus. This is the case with evolution.

Because the term *evolution* is used in so many ways, many of them inappropriate, we will define it briefly here so we know what we are talking about, and elaborate on the definition in the following pages. Evolution as a formal theory contains a set of simple, interlinked propositions:

1. All current species have descended from common ancestors. Just as all humans alive today are descended from an increasingly smaller group of previous humans, so all mammals are descended from an earlier group, and all vertebrates from an earlier group of vertebrates, and all animals from an earlier group and so on. Ultimately, all the life that has ever existed on earth is descended from a single-celled life form that lived almost four billion years ago.
2. Changes in species occur gradually over time as a consequence of mutations—small chemical changes in our DNA that are constantly occurring. Most mutations are irrelevant; many are harmful, but some are beneficial and enhance the reproductive success of their hosts.
3. Species change when beneficial mutations allow certain of them to have more offspring than others. Because the mutation results in more offspring, it spreads throughout the population and comes to dominate.

This, in a nutshell, is the theory of evolution. Note that it does *not* deal with the origin of life; whether chemicals can combine to produce life is not a part of the theory of evolution, although it is an interesting scientific question. It also does not say anything about whether the processes that drive it have purpose. Such questions are theological, not scientific.

The percentage of scientists who reject evolution is very small—so small that in most large gatherings of scientists you would not find even one person who rejects the theory of evolution. And almost all Christian biologists accept evolution as well.

Critics of evolution challenge these claims. You may have heard that "many scientists are abandoning evolution" or that "a large number of scientists have publicly repudiated evolution." The Worldview Weekend organization, for example, states confidently that evolution is receiving "fatal" blows and will soon die. "Like a cat whose nine lives are running out, evolution is, bit by bit, discovery by discovery, coming to a point of total demise."[1] We find this claim quite remarkable, as we are unaware of a single discovery any time in the last decade that, even with great exaggeration, could be described as "fatal."

The author goes on to make the even more extraordinary claim: "Few premier scientists any longer believe in Darwin's evolution," and that eventually only the "terminally stubborn will accept evolution."[2] We wonder about the basis for this statement. Just as we are unaware of any "fatal blows" that evolution has received, we are equally unfamiliar with any premier scientists who reject evolution. There are certainly a few scientists who reject evolution, just as there are scientists who reject relativity, big bang cosmology, quantum mechanics or that HIV causes AIDS and every other mainstream scientific idea. There are even a couple of "scientists" who reject the sun-centered model of the solar system, insisting that the earth does not move. But these are never premier scientists.

Unfortunately, these claims abound within the anti-evolutionary literature and are repeated so often by so many different and apparently credible people that it is easy to be misled. These claims are simply false. They are not mere "differences of opinion." They are aimed at laypeople unfamiliar with science and the scientific community, which is why they can take root and flourish. Scientists, for example, are constantly refining the details of evolution, but they are *not* abandoning it. If they were, this would be newsworthy and would circulate both informally in the scientific community and in the trade publications that report on developments in science. The scientists at the BioLogos Foundation are unaware of *any* biologists who have abandoned evolution in the past few years. Not one.

As for those scientists who publicly repudiate evolution or express concerns about it, there is indeed a famous list called "Dissent from Darwin" where more than five hundred "scientists" have signed the following statement: "We are skeptical of claims for the ability of random mutation and natural selection to account for the complexity of life. Careful examination of the evidence for Darwinian theory should be encouraged."[3]

This claim, at first glance, is an impressive and effective piece of anti-evolutionary public relations. Surely such widespread dissent must indicate that something is wrong with evolution. But let's look closer.

For starters, there are problems with the list itself. Many of the scientists listed are not trained in biology and so are not in a position to evaluate the central theory of that field. Of the two authors of this book, only one is a trained biologist capable of speaking with authority about evolution. The other is a trained physicist, who took his last biology course in 1975 in high school. When scientists comment on developments in fields they have not studied, they have no real authority. The "Dissent from Darwin" list includes philosophers, physicists, engineers, mathematicians and academics from other fields. Many of them never took even a single course in biology beyond high school. No doubt they are sincere in their views, but do we need to take their concerns about evolution seriously?

Many names on the list are of emeritus professors from various institutions. *Emeritus* is a recognition that institutions bestow on faculty when they retire, typically around age seventy to seventy-five. Seventy-five-year-old emeritus professors would have finished most of their education a half-century ago, before the developments of the past few decades provided so much support for evolution. The presence of so many emeritus faculty on this list is another red f lag, alerting us to the fact that these "dissenters" are not active members of the scientific community.

A list of over five hundred names may seem significant and, were they all gathered in one place, the group would be impressive. But the scientific community is huge, and this group represents an insignificant fraction of the whole. To show just how truly insignificant this list is, an organization called the National Center for Science Education created a parody list of scientists who were "evolution supporters" and who were all named Steve! Despite the fact that only 1 in 100 scientists is named Steve, this list has over a thousand names on it, and most of them are working biologists, which is not true of the Dissent from Darwin list.[4]

We also note that the statement in question does not really indicate repudiation of evolution. Even enthusiastic evolutionists don't all believe that "random mutation and natural selection" are the only relevant explanatory elements in evolution. Merely expressing skepticism about the adequacy of these two features of evolution to explain everything is hardly equivalent to repudiating the theory; in fact it's not even genuine dissent from evolution as it is understood today in the biological community.

And, finally, scientific truth is not decided by the number of names on a list, or who wins the debate or convinces the most people. It is based on *evidence.*

There is a scientific method, and the ideas that are widely accepted are those that have met criteria for being strongly supported by evidence and consistent with the rest of science. In all cases the validity of scientific ideas is best addressed by the leading experts who understand those ideas most thoroughly.

Any time the authority of a scientist is invoked we should check to see if the scientist is an authority on the topic on which they are speaking. In addition, we should consider whether they are simply using the authority of the scientific community to support a position on which they are no better informed than a layperson. Expertise matters.

For these and other reasons we suggest that the opposition to evolution has been greatly exaggerated. The evangelical literature is so filled with misrepresentations and outdated information about evolution that even a lot of research might not lead an honest seeker to the truth. We caution that Christians should take no comfort in the misplaced hope that the scientific community is gradually abandoning the theory of evolution. The case is quite the opposite.

So What Is Evolution?

Evolution in the most general sense—not the narrow technical sense we introduced earlier—means simply "change over time." For example, we can say that iPods have *evolved* over the past few years; they have gotten smaller, hold more songs and no longer use disk drives to store the music. This is one use of the word *evolve.* But when scientists use the term, sometimes imprecisely despite the fact that they should know better, they refer to the entire history of life on earth and sometimes even the entire history of the universe from the big bang to the present.

Biological evolution, our topic here, refers to the way that species from the past developed into the diverse roster of species that exist today.[5] This incredibly slow process takes millions and even billions of years, a time frame beyond our comprehension, which is one reason why so many people have trouble understanding evolution. Not even scientists have an intuitive feel for millions of years.

Evolution in the sense of "change over time" is displayed clearly in the fossil record, where stacked geological layers reveal a progressively changing roster of animals and plants as we move from ancient to more modern strata. There are many layers with absolutely no human fossils in them, for example. And then, in more recent layers, humanoid fossils appear. By the time humanoid fossils appear in the record there are no more dinosaur fossils. We can thus infer, quite reasonably, that dinosaurs flourished during an era when there were no humans, but dinosaurs went extinct and millions of years later humans appeared. Many less dramatic changes are displayed as well, including animals developing feathers from ancestors with scales, or animals that lived on land adapting to living in the water and gradually losing their limbs. All this is clear from the fossil record.

What Is the Role of Genes?

The physical features of animals and plants are based, in large part, on their genes, which guide the development of the organism throughout its life. Genes are the fundamental units of heredity and are made of DNA, the famous molecular double helix that unzips and copies itself in the reproductive process. The molecules that make up DNA are arranged in a long chain. They have some flexibility to change and move around, more or less randomly, which modifies the chain in unpredictable ways. These changes alter the genes which, of course, changes the instructions that the genes provide to guide the development of the organism.

Modifications to DNA are called mutations. These mutations change the biology of the organism, sometimes in important ways, but most often in irrelevant ways not much different than when we pull a book from our bookcase and put it back in a different spot. Readers of this book have mutations in their genomes of which they are not even aware. In fact, each of us has about one hundred mutations that arose for the first time in us. Each of these mutations represents a tiny experiment.

Sometimes mutations are beneficial. They might make the organism more attractive to the opposite sex, making it easier to find mates and reproduce—or they might lay eggs that are less fragile or better camouflaged from predators. Changes like these are *favorable* to the production of offspring, and organisms with these "new and improved" features will have more offspring than their old-fashioned peers. In this way a disproportionate number of the new genes will be passed on to the next generation.

Often mutations are harmful. If a bird has a mutation causing it to lay eggs that are too fragile, for example, the eggs may break open too soon and none of the hatchlings will survive. A mutation like this interferes with successful reproduction, and since the offspring that possess it won't survive, these mutations will generally be eliminated in the population.

If a population of some species undergoes a substantial number of such changes, it can eventually turn into a new species, a process called *speciation.* Usually speciation requires that the population be geographically isolated from other related populations so that the beneficial genes do not get diluted among the entire population. Mutations in the human species, for example, can easily spread among the entire population. But if everyone from, say, Canada, moved to the moon, then mutations in that population could eventually, over millions of years, lead to a new species that would be unable to breed with the parent species on earth. The new species would not necessarily be more advanced in any meaningful sense; it might even be less advanced according to some criteria. But it would be different.

Species change slowly, so these processes are, for practical purposes, invisible. Even over the course of a millennium a species with a reproductive cycle like humans would typically not change in any noticeable way. Our knowledge that species have changed dramatically over time does not come from watching them. Nevertheless we do have great confidence that all of today's species have descended from ancestral forms that no longer exist. We can go further in fact and claim that all related species—canines, for example—descended from a single common ancestor.

What Is Common Descent?

A central principle of biological evolution is that all living things descended from earlier and usually simpler life forms known as ancestral species. Just as you and your cousins have a common grandparent ancestor from whom you all descended, so many species share a common ancestor. Evidence found in ancient rocks suggests that these organisms first appeared on earth about 3.85 billion years ago. These organisms, just tiny single cells with no hard parts to fossilize, left only indirect clues to their existence, shrouding the origin of life in mystery.

The origin of life remains unexplained, and we will talk about the significance of this later. For now we simply note that most evolutionary theorists consider the origin of life to be outside the scope of biological evolution. The theory of evolution, after all, is a theory about how *life* has changed over time; it is *not* a theory about how life first appeared.

These original organisms, however they originated, carried information and were capable of self-replication—making copies of themselves. Over long periods of time the reproductive enhancements powered by beneficial mutations—as well as nature's selection against detrimental mutations—led to the diversity of living things today. This is the theory of evolution in a nutshell—the BioLogos worldview—and the grand story of the creative world that God brought into existence.

In *The Origin of Species,* Darwin made the common observation that the offspring of any species differ only slightly from their parents. Although Darwin did not know it at the time, these physical differences are a consequence of variation in the DNA of the organism. The changes that appear in a single generation—the ones that make us look different from our parents—are usually due to a simple reshuffling of preexisting genetic variations and not to any brand new features. Darwin was remarkably insightful in figuring out how this worked without knowing about genes.

Over time mutations in DNA can produce novel features, as we noted earlier, like feathers from scales or eyes from light-sensitive pigment. These mutations in the DNA subtly favor certain features, although they appear to develop randomly. The process, however, is not a random process, nor should it be described as purposeless. Since almost all organisms live in environments that change—sometimes dramatically—there needs to be a mechanism for those organisms to "hunt" for variations that will keep them adapted to these changing environments. If, for example, the weather grows colder, then the copying process that specifies the thickness of the fur will be more effective if random variations enable it to "explore" the possibility of making the fur thicker. In the event that the process, over many generations, finds a way to do this with the right mutation, that mutation will confer a great advantage on the offspring who inherit it. This advantage will lead to enhanced reproduction, and soon the instructions for how to make thicker fur will come to dominate the species. We emphasize that there is nothing random about an organism that is better adapted to its environment having greater reproductive success. This is an orderly and predictable trajectory in the direction of better adaptation.

Most people cannot conceptualize this aspect of evolution because the changes are so slow and the time frames too long for our imagination. Just as watching a blade of grass for an hour provides no evidence that it is growing, so watching a species over a human lifetime provides no evidence that it is evolving. But grass grows, species evolve, and nature continues to surprise.

What Is Natural Selection?

Darwin emphasized the struggle of species to survive and reproduce. Throughout nature, plants and animals compete for life-sustaining resources, from water to sugar to sunlight. They struggle to avoid becoming the nourishment for other organisms. They struggle to find mates to have offspring with. The variations an organism brings into the world can help or hinder in these struggles, and natural selection will help spread them or eliminate them via differential reproduction. This is one of the ways that nature protects species from becoming weak and dysfunctional.

Assessing the significance of a mutation, however, is not as simple as it might appear. Changes that are beneficial in one setting might not be as positive in another. The genetic instructions that specify the thickness of polar bear fur might get altered so the fur ends up being thicker. In an especially cold climate this would be an advantage; in a warm climate it would be a disadvantage. And some mutations, like the one in the gene for hemoglobin that causes sickle-cell anemia, have both positive and negative effects at the same time.

Sickle-cell anemia is a blood disorder that causes red blood cells to assume an abnormal sickle shape. This reduces their flexibility and leads to complications that reduce life expectancy to less than fifty years. About 1 in 500 black children in the United States is born with this disease; almost no white children have it. One third of the inhabitants of sub-Saharan Africa have the gene. How did this happen, and what is the basis for the racial disparity?

The mutation that causes sickle-cell anemia also protects against malaria, an advantage of enormous significance in climates where malaria is common, like Africa. Historically, this mutation was of great reproductive value and thus spread widely throughout the populations of Africa. In northern climates, where malaria was rare, the mutation is a disadvantage.

For a trait to be genuinely beneficial it must confer some reproductive advantage, enabling its possessor to have more offspring—this is the basic rule of evolution. Such a benefit spreads through a population, since organisms with the benefit produce more offspring. This is often called the "struggle for survival" or even the "survival of the fittest," but, as we can see from the polar bear and sickle-cell examples, often there is no real struggle involved. In any case, enhancing reproduction is the method nature uses to "select" certain traits. Darwin called this process "natural selection," the term we still use.

Scientists have recently proposed that natural selection is not based solely on the struggle for survival of *individual* organisms. After all, organisms rarely live solitary lives—fish live in schools, birds in flocks, bees in hives, humans in tribes, professors in ivory towers. Such groups of organisms benefit from their members doing things for the good of the group—even things that might sometimes be detrimental to the individual. A bird, for example, might chirp a warning that a cat is approaching, calling attention to itself but giving its flockmates time to escape. Flocks with birds that do this will be more successful than those where individuals look out only for themselves. This is called "group selection" because it considers the survival needs of an entire community of a given species.

The challenges that communities—human and otherwise—face create pressures for the members of the communities to cooperate for the good of the whole. Nature does not merely select or reward selfish behavior. High reproduction rates, for example, are normally advantageous for the evolution of a species whose members live in relative isolation. However, for a species living in community, high reproduction rates can lead to problems like a diminishing food supply or the flourishing of predators. Such communities are more likely to flourish if their members have modest reproduction rates.

When Did Genetics Become a Part of Evolution?

The inheritance of genetically based characteristics—physical, social, psychological—is the crux of natural selection. Significant change over time simply cannot occur if beneficial traits are not passed on from generation to generation.

When Darwin published *The Origin of Species,* inheritance was quite mysterious. Darwin had a profoundly wrong view called "blending," in which traits from both parents would be blended or averaged in offspring. His critics noted, correctly, that such blending would lead every characteristic to move quickly back to the average value for the species, thus dissipating any advantages from the surprise appearance of a beneficial trait.

Decades later the rediscovery of Mendel's work on genes explained, with impressive mathematical specificity, how inheritance worked. But Mendel's research was not synthesized with evolution until the middle of the twentieth century. Virtually all of the critiques of evolution prior to this synthesis, such as those of William Jennings Bryan (1860-1925), the famous lawyer who prosecuted John Scopes in Dayton, Tennessee, were swept away by the compelling nature of this synthesis. Genetics and natural selection now combined to provide a more complete and satisfactory theory of evolution called "Neo-Darwinism."[6] Calling evolution "Darwinism," as so many of its critics like to do, is really a misnomer since so much has happened since *The Origin of Species* was published.

Over the past half century, evolution has united the various subdisciplines within biology into a coordinated whole. Where once there were unrelated scientific investigations in specialized areas, including paleontology, comparative anatomy, genetics, ecology and cell biology, all these areas are now united under the broad explanatory umbrella of evolutionary biology. The famous Eastern Orthodox biologist Theodosius Dobzhansky captured the significance of this synthesis when he said, in an oft-quoted phrase, "Nothing in biology makes sense except in light of evolution."[7]

What Is the Best Proof That Evolution Has Occurred?

Immediately after Darwin published *The Origin of Species* in 1859, the consequences for human origins and biblical interpretation were apparent. The potential disparity between the Genesis creation story and Darwin's theory leads people to assume the church at the time felt threatened and opposed evolution. But many church leaders in the late nineteenth century actually embraced Darwin's theory as an insight into the means God used to create the world. For example, the conservative Christian theologian B.B. Warfield wrote, "I am free to say, for myself, that I do not think that there is any general statement in the Bible or any part of the account of creation, either as given in Gen. I & II or elsewhere alluded to, that need be opposed to evolution."[8]

The idea that humans might be related to the great apes was not universally well received, however. The wife of the bishop of Worcester, England, upon hearing this news, reportedly responded with some alarm: "Descended from the apes? My dear, let us hope that it is not true," she said. "But if it is, let us pray that it will not become widely known."

Now, 150 years later, we are still fighting this battle. A recent Gallup poll indicates that 44 percent of people in the United States believe God created humans in their present form fewer than ten thousand years ago. This belief grows more untenable with each passing day.

The mapping of DNA has enabled our understanding of human origins to achieve a level of detail Darwin never could have imagined. The decoding of the entire DNA sequence of humans—the Human Genome Project—along with the genomes of many other vertebrates has established conclusively that the data fits a model of evolution from a common ancestor. Although some still argue that DNA similarities do not prove common ancestry—God might have reused the same DNA patterns for similar animals—the details have even ruled out that conclusion.

Most mammals, for example, do not need dietary sources of vitamin C because they can make their own. But primates, including humans, require vitamin C in their diet, or they will suffer a disease called scurvy. What happened? The human genome has a degenerated copy of the gene that makes the enzyme for synthesizing vitamin C. This "broken" gene has lost more than half of its coding sequence. To claim that the human genome was created by God independently, rather than having descended from a common ancestor, means God inserted a broken piece of DNA into our genomes. This is not remotely plausible.

The last few years have seen many comparisons of our own genome to that of other species—all completely consistent with an evolutionary explanation. Recent work on Neanderthals' DNA has been pieced together from several thirty-thousand-year-old bones of different Neanderthal individuals. The DNA similarity to *Homo sapiens* is striking.

Humans are a lot alike at the DNA level. But if you compared your DNA sequence to your neighbors', about one in every thousand letters of the code would be different. These differences are common in the human population, and most are in parts of the genome that tolerate variation. They don't have much effect. But, since they can be handed down across the generations, they are interesting reflections of our history.

This history connects us to the Neanderthals. Some of the variations we carry are also found in Neanderthals, whose genomes are now being mapped. Precise but unusual variations are found both in our DNA and in the DNA from Neanderthal bones. The data imply two interesting evolutionary connections. The first connection reveals that Neanderthals and homo sapiens shared a common ancestor about a million years ago. There are specific genetic markers that we share with the Neanderthals that both of us inherited from this common ancestor.

The second connection relates to the fact that the Neanderthals went extinct 30,000 years ago after a period of interbreeding with those humans that migrated out of Africa. The continuing presence of Neanderthal DNA in non-Africans provides evidence of common ancestry for many human groups from this era of interbreeding. Since Neanderthals and humans were able to interbreed this technically means that they were not a separate species. Neanderthals are perhaps best understood as a subspecies of homo sapiens. Compelling evidence of this sort for common ancestry grows almost daily.

Can Evolution Really Make New Species?

Nearly everyone agrees that small scale, or micro, evolution is an uncontroversial fact. We know of nobody who challenges this because there are so many examples, like bacteria constantly evolving new defenses against antibiotics. But bacteria's capacity to evolve defenses against penicillin, while certainly a big deal for the bacteria and the pharmaceutical industry, hardly compels us to accept that this process can turn a reptile into a bird or a land animal into a whale. This process, called "macroevolution," appears impossible, even absurd, to many people.

Critics of macroevolution note that, despite centuries of observation, no new species have been directly observed coming into existence.[9] If evolution is such a well-established fact, why is the natural world not filled with species in the process of turning into something else—fish growing legs, reptiles sprouting feathers, humans improving in some way? Scientists have observed only relatively unimpressive variations among preexisting species, or microevolution, like the variations in finch beaks in the Galapagos Islands or the variation of dogs' body types in societies that breed them.[10]

In the case of dogs, to take a familiar example, we are certainly impressed by the difference between a dachshund and a Great Dane, but at the end of the day they are still both dogs, just as they were at the beginning of the day. Heroic breeding efforts—patiently accumulating gradual changes across centuries—have provided nothing more than new forms of the same species. There is a natural commonsense intuition that species are, on average, stable and unlikely to evolve into new species. So, while small, microevolutionary changes certainly occur, there seems to be limited evidence for large-scale, macroevolutionary changes. Scientists, however, make the confident claim that macroevolution is simply microevolution writ large: add up enough small changes and we get a large change. So what is really going on here?

The important, appropriate and entirely reasonable question to ask is, Does the uncontroversial fact of *microevolution* provide evidence for the complex and controversial claims of *macroevolution?* In fact, we believe this particular question is really at the heart of the entire controversy over evolution.

We begin our response by noting that the distinction between *micro* and *macro* evolution is arbitrary. Every step along an evolutionary pathway is, in fact, a tiny, *micro,* evolutionary change. A mother reptile cannot produce baby birds, pre-human primates cannot have human babies, and fish cannot generate legs in one generation.

Consider a familiar analogy: nobody could have imagined how Henry Ford's primitive Model T automobile could have turned into Toyota's Prius hybrid. Such dramatic changes would have been inconceivable; it would have been impossible for the engineers at Ford to develop all the remarkable engineering necessary to turn a Model T into a Prius in one model year. The electronic enhancements alone took decades to invent and develop. But if we line up a century of cars, the picture looks very different. The gap between a Prius and a Camry is not that great, nor is the gap between a Camry and the first Mustang. When you collect all the small changes you get a transformation so large it could hardly have been imagined by a science fiction writer. And yet we could certainly imagine a critic ridiculing the idea that steady improvements in the Model T concept would one day lead to a Prius. We have to distinguish between *challenges to our imaginations,* which have trouble conceptualizing slow processes that take millions of years, and *challenges to nature,* which have no such limitations.

The emergence of a new species through macroevolution, a process called *speciation,* involves nothing more than a long series of microevolutionary changes within a subgroup of a species. In a typical speciation scenario a "daughter" population of, say, wolves would get separated from its parent population, perhaps by an avalanche that might block a pathway between two valleys, or a flood that might create a new river dividing a region. The daughter population, initially identical to the parent group, will experience microevolutionary changes in an environment that, in all likelihood, will be slightly different from that of the parent. There may be, for example, different predators or less abundant water, and these differences would make fitness in the daughter population different than in the parent population. Natural selection and genetic drift would thus pull the species in a different direction in the new population.

Microevolutionary changes in the daughter population derive from small changes in the DNA of that group. Each small change in the DNA makes it harder for members of the daughter group to breed with members of its original parent population. After all, the incredibly long strands of DNA of two organisms have to unite successfully to produce healthy offspring. As changes between the two groups accumulate, they become significant enough to prevent interbreeding. According to the previous definition of species, this means a new species has evolved. Now, even if the daughter and parent populations mix again, there will be no interbreeding and genetic changes unique to each group will be preserved.

What would the just-described process look like over the course of millions of years? Initially there would be one large population of wolves, in this example. These wolves would live in a specific area and be constantly exchanging DNA by breeding with one another. A small subset of these wolves would suddenly be separated, as described, by some sort of change to the landscape. They would then evolve on their own, in a slightly different environment. A million years later this barrier would disappear and a new wolf-like species from nearby would enter the habitat of the original wolves. It would not be immediately clear that the new group had evolved from the old one. There would not be, for example, the roster of transitional forms making smooth connections from one to the other; most species—especially the short-lived intermediates—go extinct without leaving any fossil traces. No doubt some observers would ridicule the suggestion that the two groups were related, just because they had similarities.

We don't observe such macroevolutionary changes because they take such a long time, often millions of years, and they leave very uneven records. We don't see these changes, quite simply, because we cannot watch long enough.[11] Furthermore, genetic mutations that contribute to macroevolutionary changes are rare (most mutations are irrelevant), which accounts for both the slow pace of evolutionary development and the remarkable long-term stability of species once they appear.

Macroevolution typically cannot be expedited by selective breeding. To breed dogs with dogs, for example, will result mainly in a reshuffling of information already present within the canine genes of that population. To get a new species there has to be new genetic information, which typically is produced only by genetic mutations over long periods of time. Certain traits, like extremes of size or color or personality that are already present within the genes, can be selectively bred for. Such breeding can make those features more prevalent within the population and can certainly lead to dogs that look and act very different. Selective breeding, however, does not accelerate the rate at which genetic mutations occur. Because these novel mutations are essential for macroevolution, selective breeding will not speed up the process of macroevolution. There is thus no significance whatsoever to the claim that centuries of selective breeding have failed to produce a new species. Selective breeding can no more produce new species than it can produce geese laying golden eggs.

Is There Proof of Macroevolution?

Immediately after Darwin published *The Origin of Species* in 1859, the consequences for human origins emerged, quite naturally, as the most troubling part of his far-ranging theory. The idea that humans might be related to the great apes was disturbing.

The study of DNA, which began many decades after Darwin, has enabled our understanding of human origins to achieve a level of detail Darwin never could have imagined. The decoding of the entire DNA sequence of humans—the Human Genome Project, which one of the authors of this book had the privilege of leading—along with the genomes of dozens of other vertebrates has been a rigorous test of whether the data actually fits a model of evolution with countless macroevolutionary transitions from common ancestors.

The evidence for macroevolution that has emerged in the past few years is now overwhelming. Virtually all geneticists consider that the evidence proves common ancestry with a level of certainty comparable to the evidence that the earth goes around the sun. Some critics, however, still argue that DNA similarities do not prove common ancestry. Their argument is that God might have used the same DNA patterns for animals of anatomic similarity, just as a car manufacturer might use common components for different cars. This would make sense if the component—say, the knobs on the radio—were perfectly suited for a function that was identical from one car to the next. And certainly radio knobs would be in this category. The details of the analysis of DNA, however, make that conclusion implausible when applied to genomes. The genomes of organisms do not merely share common genes that successfully perform their intended functions. Genomes also share genes that are broken. By analogy, we certainly would *not* expect that a car company, having discovered that the radio knobs on their compact cars won't turn in cold weather, would decide to use the same defective knobs on all their cars. The example of the broken vitamin C gene that we looked at earlier is a case in point.

Mountains of data arrive on a daily basis as more genomes are mapped, providing compelling evidence for macroevolution. This data, however, does not specify, by itself, *how* those changes occurred, *when* they occurred or *how long* they took. Other information is needed to address those questions. The genome data could be compared to photographs you have collected over the years that show you in different locations. Here you are at the Eiffel Tower on your honeymoon; there you are at Niagara Falls with teenage children; and now you are in your house reading this book while a picture of your grandchildren sits above you on the mantle. Photographs like this prove that you traveled from the Eiffel Tower to Niagara Falls to your home, in that order, but they provide few details beyond that.

The most interesting macroevolutionary changes, at least from the perspectives of the writers and readers of this book, are those that lead to us, of course. The data already discussed align with evidence from fossils and other sources, providing clear evidence for how this occurred. The most interesting question in all of this, however, is how we are related to other animals that exist today and what implications that has for how we understand ourselves.

Did We Come from Monkeys?

Like all life on this planet, we share a common ancestry with other species, but we did not come from monkeys or any other presently existing species. Rather than having evolved from chimps or any other primates, humans share a common ancestor with them. The chimps are thus more like our distant cousins than our grandparents. However, unlike human family trees that reveal relevant ancestry over a manageable time scale of a few centuries, our evolutionary family tree takes us back into an unimaginably ancient past.

It would be a serious mistake to fret over this relationship if discovering monkeys on your family tree seems demoralizing. Time has created an enormous gulf between us and any ancestors we share with other primates. The popular quip "You may have come from a monkey, but I didn't" misses the point: no human came from a monkey, and any pre-human ancestor on our family tree is buried so far back in time that we need not lament the existence of these ancient relatives or be insulted at the suggestion that we are related to them. Few of us would be alarmed to discover that our family tree includes cavemen who never bathed and dragged their wives around by their hair. Our connection to these long gone ancestors is so tenuous that we would consider it irrelevant. The same is true of our primate relatives.

Our usual concept of "ancient," however, has no relevance in this context. When we speak of ancient Greece or ancient languages, we are referring to things so recent that, from an evolutionary point of view encompassing billions of years, they may as well be contemporary with us. Many analogies have been invoked to make sense of this: if the history of the earth is a twenty-four-hour day, then we—and the ancient Greeks—have been here for the last few seconds; if the history of the earth is the Eiffel Tower, human history is the paint on the very top. But all such analogies fail because ultimately they ask us to conceptualize something almost as far beyond our mental capacities as the nature of God. Much of the opposition to evolution, unfortunately, is driven by our inability to imagine such vast time frames, so we are inclined to both ridicule and reject them.

In the context of human evolution, we have an odd relationship to the natural history of life on this planet. We read in Genesis, for example, that everything reproduces "after its kind," and anti-evolutionists often argue that this is incompatible with evolution.[12] But this objection is crushed by the staggering weight of the seemingly endless time intervals involved. We know from experience that species do not reproduce "after their kind" in the sense that offspring are identical clones of their parents. Such offspring *always* have tiny differences when compared to their parents. Nevertheless, despite these tiny differences, the reproductive process reliably produces offspring of the same "kind." No hospital need employ zoologists to identify the new creatures appearing each day in their maternity wards.

The tiny differences that separate children from their parents rarely give us pause. Mary's hair may be redder and Johnny's nose longer than that of their parents, but who cares? However, how different would Mary and Johnny be if we multiplied the differences by a factor of a thousand? A million? Ten million? All that evolution requires is enough generations to accumulate the sort of tiny differences that separate offspring from their parents and almost any transformation can be achieved.

From the time of the first cell down to the present, life forms have been reproducing "after their kind," but natural selection, through differential reproduction, has been sifting the countless small changes, editing the results and producing the grand diversity that we encounter today. But this has all been happening so slowly that each generation experiences a world that seems constant, free from disruptive change, predictably manageable and with almost no evidence that evolution is occurring.

The unimaginable past, with its seeming magical powers, has been dubbed "deep time."[13] Its discovery over the course of the eighteenth and nineteenth centuries was the first major scientific achievement after the Copernican and Newtonian revolutions established the motion of the earth about the sun and the explanation for that motion. Just as the discoveries in astronomy revealed a world that was so large we could no longer grasp its size, so the discovery of deep time revealed a world so old we could no longer imagine its duration.

The age of the earth, like the evolution of life on its surface, is another controversial topic we now turn to.

2

Can We Really Know the Earth Is Billions of Years Old?

By the seventh day God had finished the work he had been doing; so on the seventh day he rested.

GENESIS 2:2

A mountain of scientific data supports the idea that the earth is around 4.5 billion years old.[1] This data comes from many different sources that all converge on the same value. Many scientists believe that the age of the earth is as well-established as its motion around the sun. And once the age of the earth is accepted it is but a small step to understand that the universe is about three times older than the earth, or about fourteen billion years old.

As we noted earlier, polls show that many, and probably most, Christians in the United States believe that the earth and the universe are about ten thousand years old.[2] Much of the evangelical literature on this topic confidently claims that the great antiquity of the earth simply cannot be established by scientific measurements with any confidence. They claim the age of the earth depends not on data but on our starting assumptions. Anti-evolutionists argue that the secular scientific community arrives at the conclusion that the earth is billions of years old because they start with the assumption that there is no God, not because the data takes them there.

These bold claims are hard to justify. Nowhere does the Bible identify the age of the earth as ten thousand years, nor does it provide information that would let us infer this indirectly with any confidence. Young earth creationists often appear to be reading an anti-evolutionary agenda into the Bible and forcing it to fit assumptions they bring to the text. When the text admits of multiple interpretations they often insist on the one that maximizes the conflict with evolution.[3] They do not simply assume the Bible is true and go from there. Virtually all leading evangelical biblical scholars reject the claim that the age of the earth can be determined from the Bible.[4] They are quick to note the importance of understanding biblical Hebrew to read the Genesis creation stories appropriately and caution against assuming that our modern scientific concerns are being addressed in any way by this ancient text.

Similarly, the great age of the earth is not connected in any way to the assumption of atheism. The great antiquity of the earth was originally inferred from research done in the eighteenth century by Christian geologists, decades before Darwin, and was then refined throughout the nineteenth and twentieth centuries by further discoveries. There are now no scientific arguments of any consequence that point to the earth being just a few thousand years old. Not one isolated piece of nontrivial data, in any form, points in this direction.

The age of the earth is, of course, an important fact to be determined by careful analysis of evidence. It is not something to be settled by opinion polls, debates or rhetorical contests on the Internet. If you believe that there are true statements that can be made—as almost all Christians do—then the age of the earth has a correct value to be determined by honestly sorting through all the relevant data.

In the following pages we present uncontroversial and straightforward scientific evidence that the correct age for the earth is billions of years.

How Can We Know the Universe Is Billions of Years Old When Nobody Was There to Record This Information?

Scientists have great confidence that the earth is around 4.6 billion years old and the universe around twelve to fourteen billion years old because several unrelated lines of evidence converge on those numbers. There are arguments from data as diverse as radioactive decay and the expansion of the universe. One of the simplest and most elegant arguments comes from asking the simple question, How long would it take the light from distant objects to travel to the earth?

We begin by considering the elementary fact that the speed of light has been experimentally measured and is constant—not infinite—and therefore takes time to reach the earth from distant objects. Consider the sun, which is about 93 million miles from the earth. Because light travels at 186,000 miles per second, it takes about eight minutes for light from the sun to reach the earth. If the sun suddenly went dark, we would not know it for eight minutes. We would be standing under what appeared to be a blinding orb when in fact it was just a big cinder. To "see" the sun is to look back into the past eight minutes. Because the distances in space are so great, we often use the speed of light to measure the distances. We say, for example, that the sun is "eight light-minutes" away. If the light from a distant object takes a year to reach the earth, we say that object is one *light-year* away.

The sun is the closest star to us, right next door in cosmic terms. The other stars, and the galaxies containing them, are much farther away. The light from these objects, despite traveling incredibly fast, takes millions and even billions of years to reach the earth. If the light has been traveling billions of years to reach the earth, then the universe must be at least that old.[5] This claim has been countered by young earth creationists who assume that God created the light beams "in transit" a few thousand years ago, at the same time he created the earth and the rest of the universe.[6] This argument appears plausible and consistent until you work out its implications.

For starters, what about stars we observe exploding that are millions of light years away? If this argument is true those stars never existed. To arrange this feat, God would have had to create a burst of light around ten thousand light-years away that would look like an exploding star. This burst of light would just now be reaching us. What would be the point of this? God can, of course, do this, but the burden of proof has to be borne by those making such peculiar claims. From a scientific point of view the exploding star *is* millions of light years away, which is why it *looks* millions of light years away. It appears to have exploded millions of years ago because that is actually when it exploded. To make the "light in transit" argument work, we have to invent an encyclopedia full of separate explanations to make sense of what we observe and why it is not the way it looks. It is far better to simply acknowledge that the universe is as it appears, rather than to propose that God created all manner of optical illusions in the heavens to fool us.

Another argument advanced by young earth creationists is that the speed of light was much greater in the past: if light went faster in the past, then it would reach the earth sooner and the universe would not need to be so old for the light to have traveled to earth. The Australian creationist Barry Setterfield has made this claim, but his argument has been analyzed and found to contain serious statistical errors.[7] These errors are so great that even his fellow creationists reject his work.[8]

The easiest way to refute this argument is to note that the speed of light is an important factor in many natural phenomena, not just the rate at which photons stream through space. The most well known of many examples is Einstein's famous formula $E=mc^2$, where "c" is the speed of light, "E" is energy and "m" is mass. If energy equals mass multiplied by the speed of light squared, then there would have been much more energy in the past than there is now. This violates the conservation of energy, which states that energy cannot be created or destroyed; it can only change form, which is what happens, for example, when chemical energy in gasoline is converted to energy of motion to move your car. The conservation of energy is the best-established law in all of science, and hypotheses that violate it are no longer taken seriously by the scientific community.

We hasten to add that God *could* have created a universe with the appearance of age. But this takes the question from science to theology. While God is certainly *capable* of creating the appearance of age, we suggest this does not align with his character or a clear reading of Genesis. We also counter that God could have created the universe ten minutes ago and implanted false memories in our minds. The question for science in a Christian context is not "What might a supernatural creator be capable of doing?" Rather, we should ask, "What does the empirical evidence suggest that a supernatural creator actually did?"

What About the Big Bang?

Another independent line of evidence for the great age of both the earth and the universe comes from the big bang, which, despite being unpopular with young earth creationists, is actually thought by many Christians to strongly support belief in God. Hugh Ross's Reasons to Believe organization and William Lane Craig both use the big bang as an apologetic argument for belief in God.[9] Whatever we might think about the big bang, however, compelling evidence supports it.

Several lines of evidence indicate that the universe began in an event called the big bang about fourteen billion years ago. Since that extraordinary moment of creation, the universe has been expanding steadily, which is how we observe it today. The expanding universe spreads out the galaxies so they grow ever farther apart as time passes with no apparent end in sight. Edwin Hubble discovered this expansion unexpectedly in 1928 as he was working on the distances to the galaxies.

If the universe is presently expanding, this means it must have been smaller in the past. And since it is not infinitely large today, it cannot have been expanding forever, which means that it must have started its expansion at some point in the past.[10]

The age of the universe can be determined by hypothetically re-running the expansion.[11] In a certain sense we exist in the midst of an ongoing universal "explosion" that we observe all around us when we look far out into space, like leaping into a lake with an inner tube and watching ripples of water moving away from us in all directions.

The present rate of expansion of the universe can be measured quite accurately. The question that arises is how long would it take for a universe of our size to get from zero to the present? The calculation is actually surprisingly simple as we can see from this analogy: Imagine driving a car at 50 miles per hour for 100 miles. A simple calculation tells us that the car has been traveling for two hours. This same logic applies to galaxies: by knowing the universe's rate of expansion and the average distance between galaxies, a simple calculation reveals how long the universe has been expanding from its original small size to its present vast size.

The physics that makes this calculation possible is remarkably simple. The speed at which the galaxies are moving can be measured using the Doppler effect—the same trick police use to check our speed by radar. The radar gun bounces radiation off your car, and if our car is moving, the motion changes the wavelength of the radiation by an amount proportional to our speed. If we are stationary, the radiation is unaffected and returns to the radar gun unchanged. Likewise, the radiation from a moving galaxy is changed in a well-defined way that lets us determine how fast it is moving. If the galaxy is moving away, its radiation has what we call a "red shift"; if it is approaching, it has a "blue shift." Hubble discovered that virtually all of the galaxies have red shifts, which means they are moving away from us.

The second part of this measurement is Hubble's surprising discovery that the farthest galaxies are moving the fastest. To establish this, Hubble needed to know how far away the galaxies are and compare this distance to their red shifts. The distance to a galaxy can be determined quite readily by comparing the *actual brightness* of the galaxy to its *apparent brightness,* as seen from earth. A bright galaxy will, of course, appear dim if it is far away, just as the headlights of an oncoming car appear dim when the car is far away.[12] The actual brightness of a galaxy—as opposed to the apparent brightness, which declines with distance—can be determined by identifying some aspect of the galaxy with a known brightness. This would be like estimating the distance to a particular car based on the fact that car headlights from that model all have similar brightness. In the same way, various types of stars can be identified that all have approximately the same brightness, no matter where they are. So just as you could, in principle, determine the distance to a car by measuring the apparent brightness of its headlights, so can you determine the distance to identical stars by measuring their brightness.

With this information the tools are in place to determine the age of the universe; the process is actually so simple that astronomy students sometimes do laboratory exercises on this topic. Recent measurements of the universe's expansion rate by the Hubble telescope indicate that the universe is twelve to fourteen billion years old. Distant galaxies must have been moving away from each other for this amount of time to be where they are.

Other techniques confirm this conclusion about the age of the universe, but they are rather involved to explain in detail. We mention one other method. Surrounding our Milky Way galaxy are more than a hundred globular star clusters. Each contains a few hundred thousand stars, bound together by their mutual gravity. These massive aggregations of stars have so much collective gravity that they have been stable since shortly after the formation of the universe, orbiting about the center of gravity of the cluster. The stars shine because of nuclear reactions in their cores that convert hydrogen into helium, under the great pressure of gravity. More massive stars shine hotter and brighter, but they also run out of nuclear fuel more rapidly. Bigger stars die sooner. In the oldest of the globular clusters the brightest stars have already burnt out. Younger globular clusters still have more of the truly luminous stars. Careful computer modeling can assign ages to the globular clusters based on the brightest surviving stars. The oldest globular clusters have ages around 12 billion years.

What is significant about all these different approaches—and there are others we have not mentioned—is that they converge on essentially the same age for the universe. If the universe is not approximately thirteen billion years old, it is hard to explain why so many independent lines of evidence lead to that same result. Readers interested in the surprising number of unrelated measurements that confirm this age for the universe can consult just about any introductory astronomy text.[13]

What About the Age of the Earth?

Measurements of the age of the earth fit nicely into the previous scenario for the age of the universe. Our sun is a "second generation" star with an age of approximately five billion years. It formed from an earlier star that exploded at the end of its life and spread material through the region of space where our solar system is today. This earlier star would have needed a few billion years to reach the point where it would explode, a typical and regularly observed fate for stars of a certain size. Our sun and the planets, including the earth, began forming from the debris of this exploded star about five billion years ago. This debris would have been rich in heavy elements that were cooked in the nuclear furnace of the earlier star. All these are things astronomers would know without even considering evidence from the planets themselves. It is thus gratifying to discover that, when we start measuring the age of the earth, it fits perfectly into this larger pattern.

Determining the age of things on the earth and even the earth itself is a much less abstract exercise than determining the age of the universe—as we might expect. There are, for example, many familiar cycles in nature that track the passage of time in ways not much more complicated than human birthdays. For instance, trees form yearly rings on their trunks, so we can determine a tree's age by counting its rings. The oldest living trees on earth are the six-thousand-year-old bristlecone pines found in the Sierra Nevada. The dead trees lying beside them are almost twice as old.[14] Similarly, lakebeds accumulate sediments with seasonal variations: minerals in spring, pollen and plant material in summer and fall. This creates distinguishable annual layers that can be counted on the bottom of lakes, just like counting tree rings or candles on a child's birthday cake. Scientists have found lakebeds with layers as old as thirty-five thousand years.[15]

The seasonal ice rings in glaciers provide another example. The ice rings form through the accumulation of years of falling snow, and we can distinguish seasonal differences—such as increased dust and larger ice crystals in summer—that allow the age to be determined. Scientists have drilled ice cores deep into the glaciers and found ice that is 123,000 years old in Greenland, and as old as 740,000 years in Antarctica.[16]

Such dating methods do not take us very far into the earth's past, but they are extremely straightforward. We simply pull a cylindrical plug from a glacier and count the layers. The clarity of this method of dating is one of the reasons why scientists react so negatively to claims that the earth is less than ten thousand years old. An ice core with 500,000 seasonal summer layers of pollen can no more be ten thousand years old than a massive oak with two hundred annual rings can be two years old.

To go back further in time we need other dating methods. One such method derives from very precise variations in the orbit of the earth, called Milankovitch cycles. These are long-term cyclic changes in climate, and in the last few hundred thousand years these cycles produced the ice ages. Analysis of the effects of these Milankovitch cycles takes us back thirty million years.[17]

Another approach is based on the reversal of the earth's magnetic field, which happens two to three times every million years for reasons not presently understood. The evidence for this is also straightforward. When molten rock pushed up from the hot interior of the earth solidifies, as is constantly happening under the ocean, the magnetic field it encounters is frozen into the rock. When magnetic material is in a molten state, all the tiny internal atomic magnets are free to move and will naturally align with the local magnetic field, like an array of tiny compass needles. When the rock solidifies, the internal structure and orientations of the tiny magnets in the rock are frozen and can be measured to determine the direction and even the strength of the magnetic field at the time of solidification.

Geologists have found solidified rocks under the ocean with their magnetic fields changing direction, back and forth, as you move out from the hotspot ridge where the rock is coming up from the interior. There will be a long ribbon of rock with the north poles in one direction, then a long ribbon with a reversal, and so on. By counting these reversals, and knowing that they occur every few hundred thousand years, we can trace the history of these rocks back 170 million years.[18]

These methods provide a lower limit for the earth's age and establish with reasonable certainty that the earth is way more than ten thousand years old, but they do not provide an upper limit. They simply cannot point further back because of limitations in measurement. Trees, for example, live for thousands of years, but not millions. Furthermore, in the case of tree rings, about 11,800 years ago at the end of the last ice age, the climate changed abruptly, and the locations of old trees underwent a major shift.[19] For sediment in lakebeds, the layers become too compressed after thirty-five thousand years and can no longer be distinguished. Therefore, in order to go back closer to the time when the earth was first formed, we need methods that take us back much further. Fortunately, radiometric methods do just that.

Can Radiometric Dating Really Tell Us the Earth Is Billions of Years Old?

The most important dating method for the earth itself, as opposed to trees, lakebeds and other objects on the surface of the earth, is based on the most remarkable of clocks hidden deep within the nucleus of many atoms. We refer to the process of *radioactivity,* of which the most familiar example is carbon dating, although there are many more examples.

To see how this works we need a brief review of elementary chemistry. Matter is composed of atoms, defined by the number of protons in their nucleus: hydrogen has one, helium has two, carbon has six and so on throughout the periodic table. In most cases the number of neutrons in the nucleus is the same as that of the protons, but there can be extra neutrons in certain cases. Since these extra neutrons do not increase the charge in the nucleus, all they basically do is add extra weight.

Different weight versions of the same atom are known as *isotopes,* which are identified by a number equal to the sum of the protons and neutrons in the nucleus. Take carbon as an example. Carbon is atom number six, because it has six protons in its nucleus. With a matching number of neutrons the total number of particles in the nucleus—the *mass number* of this particular isotope of carbon—is twelve. We write this as[12] C. But a carbon nucleus can also have one or two additional neutrons. These isotopes would have thirteen or fourteen particles in the nucleus and would be written[13] C and[14] C. All three forms of carbon have nearly identical chemical properties, but they each have a slightly different mass, due to the varying number of neutrons.

The extra neutrons in the[14] C nucleus, for reasons that have to do with the way the forces in the nucleus hold the particles together, make it unstable. They disturb a natural arrangement, ever so slightly, like a drunken guest at a well-behaved dinner party. This disturbance results in a nucleus that could be described as "wound too tightly," and as a result the nucleus will sometimes spontaneously transition into a more stable form. The drunk is tossed from the party.

A nucleus with too many neutrons solves its problem in a most remarkable way—by transforming into a different atom. It does this by having one of its neutrons turn into a proton, which remains in the nucleus, and an electron, which leaves. Take[14] C, or carbon 14, as it is called. This nuclear arrangement, with six protons and eight neutrons, is unstable so, to resolve this, one of the neutrons turns into a proton and an electron. Now the nucleus has a matching—and stable—seven-proton-seven-neutron arrangement. The *unsta-*

ble carbon atom has turned into a *stable* nitrogen atom.

Stable atoms are ones that can persist indefinitely. Many hydrogen atoms in the universe are unchanged from the way they were ten billion years ago. Although many isotopes, like carbon 12, are stable, many are not. These unstable isotopes—the radioactive ones—decay at such a fixed and predictable rate that they act like clocks, allowing us to determine the age of the rocks the radioactive isotopes are found in. The energy and particles released during the decay, when a neutron converts into a proton and an electron, can be detected with an instrument called a Geiger counter. Young rocks have lots of radioactive isotopes in them; older rocks have less. Eventually, of course, radioactivity in the universe will end, as all atoms become converted into stable isotopes.

There are many atoms with radioactive isotopes. Uranium, to take one famous example, is important for determining the age of the earth. Just as[14] C is unstable and decays into a more stable form, uranium-235 ([235] U) decays into lead-207 ([207] Pb), through a sequence of radioactive events. As time passes there will be more lead and less uranium, so we can use the relative amounts of lead and uranium—their ratio—to determine the age of a rock containing these atoms. If the earth were infinitely old, there would be no uranium-235 because it all would have been converted to lead-207.

If it were very young, hardly any would have been converted. Neither of these is the case; rocks are found with a combination of uranium and lead.

How Does the Radioactive Clock Work?

To date a rock we need to know the rate at which the uranium is being converted into lead. For radioactive decay we speak of a *half-life,* which is the time it takes for half of the material to decay from its unstable starting point to its more stable final form. If the half-life of element X is one hour, and we start with forty atoms of X, then after one hour we would have twenty atoms of X; after two hours we would have ten atoms and after three hours we would have five atoms left. In a day or so element X would be gone, and only its more stable end product would remain. Obviously element X would be useful for measuring only rocks that were a few hours old. To measure the age of the earth we need something with a much longer half-life. Fortunately, there are several such elements: the half-life of uranium-235 is 713 million years, which can be determined with a Geiger counter that detects an emission whenever a uranium atom decays.

To date a rock with this process we need to know how much uranium and lead the rock had to begin with. If we could assume the rock started out as pure uranium, then dating would be easy. If it was now half uranium, it would be 713 million years old. If it was now only one-quarter uranium, then it would be twice that old, or 1.426 billion years. Unfortunately this simple assumption is not true, for we know that such rocks do not begin as pure uranium. Instead, we must determine the initial composition of the rock. Fortunately this is easy, thanks to the way uranium and lead form in the first place.

There are two isotopes of lead: lead-207 and lead-204. The two isotopes are chemically identical: nothing distinguishes them but the number of neutrons buried deep in the nucleus. So when the rock is forming and lead is being incorporated into its composition, no preference will be shown for either isotope. The two types will be incorporated in the same relative amounts as are found in the earth's crust. However, when uranium-235 decays, it creates only lead-207; the quantity of lead-204 remains the same, since it does not decay, and no unstable isotopes turn into it. Thus, as time passes, the lead-207 will increase and the lead-204 will stay the same. The steadily increasing excess of lead-207 thus chronicles the passage of time.

We now have the information needed to date the rocks. The dates we get with this radioactive process can be confirmed and refined by comparing this result to other radioactive systems. There are, remarkably, about forty different radiometric techniques available for dating rocks, each with different half-lives. Using the uranium-lead system, the age of the earth has been determined to be about 4.566 billion years, with a margin of error around ±2 million years.[20] Although this error is large compared to human history, it is just a fraction of a percent—considerably smaller than the error that results from laying out a baseball field by pacing off the distances between the bases.

Those who believe the earth is young raise two objections. First, there is a concern about inconsistencies in the dates determined by different systems; the radioactive clocks based on different isotopes do give slightly different results. But these differences are not significant. Even a huge error resulting in a number 10 percent too low would make the earth 4 billion years old instead of 4.6 billion. This is still in a completely different ballpark than claims that the earth is thousands of years old made by those who try to date the earth using a literalist reading of the Bible. Second, some suggest that radioactive decay rates were much faster in the past, making things look older than they really are. This claim simply has no evidence of any sort to back it up. In fact, there is strong counterevidence that the rates have never changed. Radioactive decay is a nuclear event and all but impervious to change. Even at temperatures and pressures that rip the electrons off the atom, absolutely no changes in the nuclear decay rates have been observed. Additionally, all decay rates would have to undergo gigantic and tightly coordinated changes in order for a relatively young earth to appear several billion years old.

Once again we caution against supposing that God created some grand deception by coordinating a long roster of changes so that everything would point toward a false age for the earth. Why not simply assume that the age of the earth is exactly what the evidence says it is?

Doesn't the Bible Teach That the Earth Is Young?

Young and old earth creationists, BioLogos, and intelligent design leaders alike all affirm that God created everything, so in a purely literal sense we are all creationists. But the word *creationism* as it is commonly used generally refers to the belief that all life on earth is the result of direct acts of intervention on God's part. These creative acts cannot be explained by science but are described in the early chapters of Genesis.

Many Christians, especially in the past few decades in America, have become convinced that the first chapters of Genesis provide a scientific account of origins. By adding up the *begats* in the Old Testament, they believe the creation took place less than ten thousand years ago. And by choosing a particular literalist interpretation of the first chapter of Genesis, they identify the creation period as six twenty-four-hour days. This young earth creationism, as we are calling it, is held by a majority of evangelicals.

YEC starts with a "biblical framework" for creation. It then looks for scientific models that fit within this framework. Trying to create a scientific model showing the earth to be ten thousand years old is, to say the least, challenging, in light of what we have just discussed. The proponents of this view, however, interpret the Bible as teaching that the earth is ten thousand years old, so, in their view, they are accepting the challenge of showing that the Bible is scientifically reliable.

Many of the leading and better-educated creationists, like Paul Nelson, Kurt Wise and John Mark Reynolds, with doctorates from the University of Chicago, Harvard University and the University of Rochester, respectively, agree with us that the scientific evidence is against young earth creationism. Nevertheless, because they believe that the Bible teaches YEC, they hold their position in spite of the evidence and hope that new evidence will move in their favor.[21] For this reason, YEC is often called "biblical creationism," although it is certainly not the only view held by those who believe the Bible contains a scientific account of origins.

Adherents to YEC are sincere in their beliefs that this view must be held by Christians. But BioLogos respectfully proposes that YEC has taken an unnecessarily narrow view of Scripture. In the first place, we do not believe that YEC's interpretation of Genesis is correct. They make assumptions about the nature of the text at odds with what many contemporary evangelical biblical scholars, like John Walton of Wheaton College, say are legitimate. Their view is even at odds with that of St. Augustine in the fourth century, who couldn't imagine why God would use a human work week to accomplish the creation. Many biblical scholars who have studied the biblical languages and cultures insist that the YEC interpretation of Genesis is not even close to what the text is saying. The leading YEC proponents are not, in fact, biblical scholars and have limited training in the relevant biblical scholarship. Their expositions of Genesis are almost entirely based on English translations of Genesis with little consideration of what the words and concepts meant in the original Hebrew. For these and other reasons the YEC view has never succeeded in becoming *the* Christian view, and a century ago even conservative Christians were not consistently attracted to it. YEC has become mainstream for evangelicals only in the last half century.

In the second place, we do not believe that God would provide two contradictory revelations. God's revelation in nature, studied by science, should agree with God's revelation in Scripture, studied by theology. Since the revelation from science is so crystal clear about the age of the earth, we believe we should think twice before embracing an approach to the Bible that contradicts this revelation.

In chapter four, we will outline an approach to Genesis that is far more sensitive to the text itself than the approach used by YEC, which is a simple literalist reading of the English translation that doesn't even take into consideration what the original Hebrew words meant.

Old Earth Creationism: What If the Days of Genesis Were Long Periods of Time?

Like their YEC counterparts, old earth creationists (OEC) are also biblical literalists, insisting that the creation stories in Genesis are scientific accounts of origins. But because there is overwhelming evidence that the earth is billions of years old, not thousands, OEC seeks an interpretation of Genesis that does not lead to a young earth but still takes the account literally. Historically, there have been three ways to do this:

1. ***The day-age theory.*** Because there is a bit of ambiguity about what the Bible means when it uses the word *day* (Hebrew, *yom),* the day-age theory argues that the days of Genesis are long periods of unknown duration. They point to the many verses in the Old Testament where *yom* clearly does not refer to a twenty-four-hour period, like Zechariah 14:9, where we read "The Lord will be king over the whole earth. On that day there will be one Lord, and his name the only

name." Thus there can be six distinct periods of creation, where God does something specific in each one, but they are simply long periods rather than twenty-four-hour days. *Reasons to Believe* is the leading contemporary proponent of the day-age theory.

2. ***The gap theory.*** Making use of some grammatical ambiguities in the first two verses in Genesis, gap theorists argue that the first verse in Genesis refers to a creation that took place at an unknown time in the past. This creation was destroyed and the second verse in Genesis refers to God's *re*-creation after this earlier catastrophe. This view became widely known through the Scofield Reference Bible, which presented it as if it were a natural interpretation of Genesis. There are presently no major organizations promoting this view, although many people do hold it.
3. ***The framework interpretation.*** There are literary devices like rhyming, repetition and parallel constructions that offer hints that the six day account in Genesis might be constructed to make some other point than time durations. For example, perhaps the six days are six days of revelation, where God presented portions of the creation story on each day. The weekly structure is thus a framework for the *presentation* of the creation story, not a set of time intervals related to the story itself. This view is also no longer very popular.

All OEC positions hold that God's creative acts are outside the natural order of things. OEC does not accept that natural processes can produce one species from another, so they reject the idea that all species are related through the process of evolutionary descent. Every creative process in history involved God miraculously intervening in the natural order. Because the revelation of God in nature—science—suggests that God worked *through* the laws of nature rather than *outside* those laws, BioLogos rejects old earth creationism, although we certainly believe that the earth is old and that God created everything. BioLogos accepts the possibility of God-ordained miracles, of course, but looks for situations where no natural explanation could possibly apply, like the resurrection of Jesus Christ. We see no reason to insist that God must miraculously intervene to accomplish things, like the origin of species, that God could just as well do by working through the laws of nature.

BioLogos holds that God's creative activity is executed *within* the natural order, working *through* and respecting the laws of nature. We will look at the biblical issues later in detail, but for now we simply suggest that this view is consistent with how God's actions are generally portrayed in the Bible. The Old Testament is replete with stories of God using floods, winds, plagues and other natural phenomena to execute his will. Why could God not also use natural mechanisms to bring about the creation?

As this book unpacks the BioLogos perspective in more detail, we believe it will become increasingly appealing to Christian readers who would like to have a position that is both biblically based and scientifically sound. But there is one major question we should address in more detail before we begin that task.

Do We Have to Let Science Tell Us How to Interpret the Bible?

Many believe that the discovery of the great age of the earth forced Christians to abandon the traditional reading of Genesis and embrace a compromise forced on them by science. Those who continue to believe in a young earth because "the Bible tells them so" claim that they are simply being faithful to the Christian tradition, courageously refusing to be bullied by a secular scientific community. They lament that Christians who accept the great age of the earth and the universe have compromised:

> Surely all those who really believe in the God of the Bible should see that any compromise with the geologic-age system is theological chaos. Whether the compromise involves the day-age theory or the gap theory, the very concept of the geological ages implies divine confusion and cruelty, and the God of the Bible could never have been involved in such a thing as that at all.[22]

This view, however appealing on the surface, misrepresents the Christian tradition. Christians across the centuries have not been united in reading Genesis in this literal way, and the widespread insistence that it can *only* be read this way is actually a recent development dating to the publication of *The Genesis Flood* in 1961.[23]

Early Christian thinkers did not have science to help them understand the earth and its history. Nevertheless, many of them were well-educated and more than capable of discerning that the Genesis creation stories were not trying to teach about the literal history of the world. The works of many of the first Christian theologians and philosophers actually reveal an interpretation of Genesis surprisingly compatible with both the great age of the earth and Darwin's theory of evolution.

Origen, an important third-century philosopher and theologian from Alexandria, Egypt—one of the great intellectual centers of the ancient world—provides an example of early Christian thought on creation. Origen presents the main doctrines of Christianity as they were understood in these early centuries and defends them against pagan accusations. In *On First Principles,* he offers the following perspective on the Genesis creation story:

> What person of intelligence, I ask, will consider as a reasonable statement that the first and the second and the third day, in which there are said to be both morning and evening, existed without sun and moon and stars, while the first day was even without a heaven? ... I do not think anyone

> will doubt that these are figurative expressions which indicate certain mysteries through a semblance of history.[24]

Fifteen centuries before there was any scientific evidence forcing a reexamination of the Genesis creation accounts, Origen opposed the idea that the creation story should be interpreted as a literal and historical account of how God created the world.

Augustine of Hippo, a bishop in North Africa during the early fifth century, is the most influential Christian of the first millennium after St. Paul. Widely known for *The Confessions,* Augustine authored dozens of other works, several of which focus on Genesis 1–2.[25] In *The Literal Meaning of Genesis,* Augustine argues that the first two chapters of Genesis are written to suit the understanding of the people at that time.

> Perhaps Sacred Scripture in its customary style is speaking with the limitations of human language in addressing men of limited understanding.... The narrative of the inspired writer brings the matter down to the capacity of children.[26]

In order to communicate in a way that all people could understand, Augustine suggests that the creation story was told in a simpler, allegorical fashion. He also believed God created the world with the capacity to develop—a view harmonious with biological evolution.[27]

Origen and Augustine are not unique in their beliefs. Thomas Aquinas, a well-known thirteenth-century philosopher, theologian and Italian priest was interested in the intersection of secular learning and Christian theology. Most scholars rank Aquinas with Augustine, Luther and Calvin as the most influential Christian thinkers in history. If you Google "St. Thomas" you will find remarkable evidence of his significance, with countless universities, libraries and even islands named after him.

Aquinas did not fear the possible contradiction between the Genesis creation story and scientific findings, and saw no need to draw lines in the sand about how to read Genesis. Oxford University scholar William Carroll notes:

> Aquinas did not think that the opening of Genesis presented any difficulties for the natural sciences, for the Bible is not a textbook in the sciences. What is essential to Christian faith, according to Aquinas, is the "fact of creation," not the manner or mode of the formation of the world.[28]

Aquinas discusses the creation story in his masterwork the *Summa Theologica,* where he responds to a question about whether all six days of creation are actually a description of a single day, an interpretation proposed as one possibility by Augustine. Aquinas does not take sides in the debate but seeks harmony between the two views.

Aquinas, like Augustine eight centuries earlier, argues in favor of the view that God created all things with the *potential* to develop:

> On the day on which God created the heaven and the earth, He created also every plant of the field, not, indeed, actually, but "before it sprung up in the earth," that is, potentially.... All things were not distinguished and adorned together, not from a want of power on God's part, as requiring time in which to work, but that due order might be observed in the instituting of the world. Hence it was fitting that different days should be assigned to the different states of the world, as each succeeding work added to the world a fresh state of perfection.[29]

Augustine's perspective influenced just about every Christian thinker who came after him and can be seen even as late as the eighteenth century—just before Darwin published *The Origin of Species*—in the works of John Wesley. An Anglican minister and early leader in the Methodist movement, Wesley, like Augustine, thought Scriptures were written in terms suitable for their audience. He writes:

> The inspired penman in this history [Genesis] ... [wrote] for the Jews first and, calculating his narratives for the infant state of the church, describes things by their outward sensible appearances, and leaves us, by further discoveries of the divine light, to be led into the understanding of the mysteries couched under them.[30]

Wesley also argues the Scriptures "were written not to gratify our curiosity [of the details], but to lead us to God."[31] The great age for the earth and even

Darwin's theory of evolution would thus not necessarily have conflicted with the perspectives of Wesley, Augustine, Aquinas, Origen or many other important Christian thinkers in the centuries before Darwin.[32]

The century after Darwin saw the emergence of the modern fundamentalist movement, which for several decades was, surprisingly, quite comfortable with the idea that the earth was very old, contrary to widespread perceptions that the fundamentalist approach to the Bible demands a young earth view. The fundamentalist movement takes its name from an ambitious project called *The Fundamentals* published between 1910 and 1915 by the Bible Institute of Los Angeles (now Biola) that defined the fundamentals of Christianity.

The contributors to *The Fundamentals* were the leading conservative Christians at the time, men like R.A. Torrey and A.C. Dixon, united in their belief in central doctrines like the virgin birth and the resurrection of Jesus, the reality of miracles and heaven, and God as the creator of everything. But they were not united in rejecting evolution as a mechanism of creation. And there was no rejection of the scientific research that indicated that the earth was far older than ten thousand years.

William Jennings Bryan, the most important anti-evolutionist of the first half of the twentieth century, was not a young earth creationist, seeing no reason to interpret the Genesis creation account as taking place over a literal seven-day week. (This is in contrast to his caricature in the play and movie *Inherit the Wind.)* Even into the 1960s few Christians had problems with an ancient earth. Moody Press published countless books written from a fundamentalist perspective, but declined to publish *The Genesis Flood* by John Whitcomb and Henry Morris because it espoused a young earth approach to Genesis they felt was no longer of interest to Christians who had mostly accepted that the earth was very old.[33]

Unfortunately, *The Genesis Flood* struck a chord with many Christians in the United States and rallied them to the cause of young earth creationism. This position, so articulately presented in *The Genesis Flood,* seemed like the best way to simultaneously respect the Bible and fight off atheistic worldviews that were claiming support from evolution. Now most evangelicals believe the Bible teaches that the earth is young and that they must therefore reject most of modern science since so many parts of it figure into the various dating methods showing the earth to be very old. But, as we have seen in this chapter, many important leaders in the history of the church rejected this view, and it was not dominant in America until the latter part of the twentieth century.

We conclude this chapter with some wise counsel from St. Augustine:

> In matters that are so obscure and far beyond our vision, we find in Holy Scripture passages which can be interpreted in very different ways without prejudice to the faith we have received.

> In such cases, we should not rush in headlong and so firmly take our stand on one side that, if further progress in the search of truth justly undermines this position, we too fall with it. That would be to battle not for the teaching of Holy Scripture but for our own, wishing its teaching to conform to ours, whereas we ought to wish ours to conform to that of Sacred Scripture.[34]

Augustine's fourth-century reflections reveal one of the great minds of the Christian tradition wrestling with the problems we engage in this book: How do we reconcile our faith commitments with other forms of knowledge, like the insights science provides into the natural world? In a surprising number of ways, Augustine, and Aquinas after him, anticipated much of what those scholars working in the field of science and religion are struggling with today.

Controversies such as those addressed in this chapter have given rise to a wide-ranging and animated discussion of the proper way to relate science and religion. In many cases, of course, this poses no problem. There are no theological problems created by scientific explanations for why the sky is blue or grass is green. Much of science is simply independent of religion and, other than being grateful to God that the world is orderly and we are curious and capable, there really is very little engagement.

But there have always been points of serious contact, especially when new information about the natural world has forced reconsideration of biblical texts.

Augustine, for example, and others of his generation were uncomfortable with reports that there were people living below the equator—the "anti-podes," so called because their feet pointed in the opposite direction from the people in the northern hemisphere, where Augustine lived.[35] The problem arose because of the claim in the New Testament that St. Paul had preached to "every creature under heaven" (Colossians 1:23), and he couldn't possibly have traveled to the anti-podes. So, as reports of such upside-down people became more and more common, Christians had to think about what those reports of Paul's teaching ministry were really saying.

Centuries later, Christians of Galileo's generation had to rethink what the psalmist meant when he wrote that the earth "can never be moved" (Psalm 104:5), reprising the same sort of challenge that confronted Augustine. Eighteenth-century Christians had to deal with the problem of extinction and the growing awareness that entire species had lived and died before humans came along. And then nineteenth-century Christians had to wrestle with Darwin, twentieth-century Christians with the big bang, and twenty-first-century Christians with DNA evidence for the relationship between ourselves and other species.

All these challenges are part of the important ongoing dialogue between God's two books—the book of nature and the Bible. Because the book of nature is an ongoing revelation, constantly adding new books and revising existing ones, this conversation will continue to be lively and engaging. We explore it in more detail in chapter three.

3

How Do We Relate Science and Religion?

And God said, "Let there be light," and there was light.

GENESIS 1:3

Science and theology have things to say to each other since both are concerned with the search for truth attained through motivated belief.

JOHN POLKINGHORNE

The Christian tradition has always engaged the secular culture. As early as the first century we find St. Paul, in his famous Mars Hill sermon, relating his message to local Greek philosophy. Early church fathers like Origen constantly borrowed secular concepts and ideas to illuminate and extend the Christian message. Augustine's classic *City of God* was a profound meditation on the relation between the kingdom of God and the secular world (city of man). Aquinas's *Summa Theologica* was a medieval integration of Christianity with newly arrived secular Greek philosophy.

This task, particularly in the work of Aquinas, demanded a familiarity with prevailing understandings of the natural world as articulated in the natural philosophy of the day. By the nineteenth century the exploration of nature would come to be called "science," but these earlier generations of thinkers did not perceive the investigation of nature as fundamentally different than the investigation of any other area of knowledge. They assumed knowledge was a seamless whole and everything related to everything else, with revealed knowledge—revelation—functioning as the primary foundation on which reflection would take place. For thinkers like Aquinas, theology was the "queen of the sciences."

In this chapter we consider the animated conversation between science and religion as it occurs today. Our considerations will be informed by the history of this conversation, of course, but we must keep in mind that religion and science were not distinct categories of knowledge in the past. The modern compartmentalization of knowledge would seem inadequate and even peculiar to many thinkers from the past.

Do Science and Religion Have to Overlap?

We start by recognizing that *most* of science does not connect in any meaningful way to *most* of religion. The (mis)perception that science and religion constantly engage each other is created by a media in love with conflict. Every time a controversy erupts over evolution, stem cells, genetics or cosmology, the media reports that science is once again challenging religion. In such stories science is advancing in its usual way by discovering new knowledge and religion is responding in its usual way by being defensive, reactionary and protective of insights from the past. This is a misleading picture. The thousands of scientific journals that report the work of the scientific community are filled with obscure discoveries that have no meaningful connection of any sort to religion and are blissfully ignored by the media and most everyone else.

In such journals we read of new measurements of the speed of light or the mass of elementary particles, determined with new levels of precision. We read of new insights into the causes of various diseases, the ongoing advance of nanotechnology or the origin of interesting geological features on the earth and other bodies in our solar system. It is all but impossible to relate such knowledge to religion and no effort need be expended trying to do so for there is simply no point. Furthermore, the Bible is completely silent on topics like these and many others.

Christians explore these and most other scientific topics without worrying about faith implications. On some subjects, of course, the Bible does make casual, sometimes literary, reference to the natural world, such as when God is connected to thunder, whirlwinds, clouds, green pastures and lions. Such allusions also occasion no worry.

But sometimes the Bible speaks with reasonable clarity about the natural world, and it is here that problems arise. In Psalm 93 we read: "The world is firmly established; it cannot be moved." This is not a passage readily dismissed as a literary device, and in fact, it occasioned great consternation in the seventeenth century when Galileo tried to convince his fellow Christians that the earth was not fixed but moved around the sun. Galileo, in the tradition of Augustine and Aquinas, struggled to reconcile the new astronomy with this venerable biblical assurance that the earth did not move. He famously quipped, "The Bible teaches us how to go to heaven, not how the heavens go," anticipating the point we made earlier, that science and religion can often avoid conflict by simply keeping them separate.

Galileo's task in the seventeenth century was like ours in the twenty-first, except we wrestle with new topics like biological evolution and the big bang, not the motion of the earth. The simple "science and religion are independent" formula, however, did not work for Galileo in his day, although thoughtful Christians today have learned to be careful not to treat Bible verses as scientific statements.

The so-called independence model for relating science and religion received a major endorsement a few years ago when the late Harvard paleontologist Stephen Jay Gould proposed it as a formula for keeping the peace. Gould, for years one of the leading public voices for science in America, argued that science and religion are so completely different that they should be viewed as separate bodies of knowledge with no relationship to each other. Gould argued that science provides empirical, factual knowledge of the world and its behavior, and religion addresses questions of values and purpose. And there is simply no overlap between these two pursuits.

Borrowing explicitly religious language, Gould labeled this view "non-overlapping magisteria," or NOMA.

> [Each] subject has a legitimate magisterium, or domain of teaching authority—and these magisteria do not overlap (the principle that I would like to designate as NOMA, or "non-overlapping magisteria"). The net of science covers the empirical universe: what is it made of (fact), and why does it work this way (theory). The net of religion extends over questions of moral meaning and value. These two magisteria do not overlap, nor do they encompass all inquiry (consider, for starters, the magisterium of art and the meaning of beauty).[1]

NOMA maps much of the relevant terrain, as we have seen, and has to be the starting point for any discussion of science and religion. We must start by understanding that we are not obliged to seek out religious meaning in the esoteric nooks and crannies of contemporary science, as if every fact about the natural world is like a fortune cookie with a little religious message inside.

Why Do So Many People Think Science and Religion Are at War?

NOMA confronts the enduring but discredited myth that science and religion have forever been in conflict. This view, known as the "warfare metaphor," originated in a pair of influential and widely read books in the nineteenth century: Andrew Dickson White's *A History of Warfare of Science with Theology in Christendom* and William Draper's *History of the Conflict Between Religion and Science.* Prior to the appearance of these books, science and religion, except for the occasional skirmish like the Galileo affair, got along fine and were actually supportive of one another, as recent scholarship has clearly shown.[2] And even the infamous Galileo affair was nothing like its urban legend. Galileo was not tortured and his so-called imprisonment was confinement to his house. There was indeed a tragic conflict, but not in the sense that polemicists like White and Draper portrayed.

Given the current highly publicized controversy over evolution, the warfare metaphor can seem all too obvious, if we forget about all the activity taking place off the media radar. In the big picture, warfare is but a minor facet of the interaction between science and religion. Unfortunately, this facet is the most interesting and, far and away, the one likely to appear in a newspaper. When creation and evolution clash in a courtroom, to take the most familiar example, the daily news fills up with stories reminding us of the supposed conflict between science and religion. There is a "Here comes the Galileo affair" template being dusted off and trotted out to make sense of the issue.

The NOMA aspect, of course, does not make the news for, alas, it is not news. Who can imagine an evening news science report beginning with, "Scientists at Yale University today announced that they have discovered the origins of dark matter. Yale theologians report that this discovery has no relevance to religion." On the other hand, we often hear stories like "Religious leaders in Kansas City have demanded a meeting with local school board officials to protest the teaching of evolution in local high schools."

Just as the majority of scientists work on topics that do not come into contact with religion, so theologians and biblical scholars pursue topics in fields unrelated to science—topics like the origins and development of Scriptures, philosophical solutions to the problem of evil and the promise of eternal life. These topics do not connect in any natural way to science. NOMA helps by highlighting the extended nonoverlapping nature of science and religion.

NOMA, however, over-compartmentalizes by equating science simplistically with factual knowledge and religion with value or opinion. In that case there would clearly be no overlap between the two pursuits, but this is true only if we accept those overly narrow and restrictive definitions.

Science is not the only source of factual statements and there are important statements made by science that are not purely factual in any simple sense. Cosmologists, for example, speak in meaningful ways about the existence of other universes, but these statements cannot be considered factual in the same sense as statements about other planets. In the same way, religion reaches beyond the realm of values and morals. If statements like "God exists" or "child abuse is wrong" are considered factual claims about reality, then, according to NOMA, they could not be religious statements. On the other hand, few scientists would consider statements like these to be scientific. So what kind of statements are they? The inability of NOMA to handle claims like these about reality highlights its limitations as a universally applicable model.

Gould acknowledged that science was limited to making factual claims about the world's physical behavior, and therefore provides only a limited picture of reality. Many however are seduced by the success of science into assuming that science is capable of discovering all possible facts about the world. The great astronomer Sir Arthur Eddington developed a winsome analogy for this assumption, describing a "man who set out to study deep-sea life using a net that had a mesh-size of three inches. After catching many wild and wonderful creatures from the depths, the man concluded that there are no deep-sea fish that are smaller than three inches in length!"[3]

NOMA, while certainly helpful and broadly applicable, is too limiting. Its definition of science breaks down at those murky theoretical boundaries where observation becomes impossible, like the claims about other universes. Likewise, religion in almost all of its manifestations is more than just a collection of value judgments and moral directives. Religion often makes claims about "the way things are."

Can Religion Contribute to Science?

Religion has been in meaningful dialogue with science for centuries. The development of modern science is a good example.

Most people, including many scholars unfamiliar with the history of ideas and bewitched by the warfare metaphor, believe that religious belief hindered the early progress of science. The disagreement between the church and Galileo is invoked to make the point, with no recognition that this was an idiosyncratic case, and not remotely representative of the times.

Recent scholarship, most of it conducted by secular academics, has established that religious belief was entirely compatible with scientific progress, even encouraging it in many cases. For example, when the top fifty-two natural philosophers during the emergence of modern science in seventeenth-century Europe were surveyed for their religious beliefs, 62 percent were labeled as devout, 35 percent as conventionally religious, and only two scientists, 3.8 percent, could be classified as skeptics.[4] Given that these thinkers laid the foundations for modern science, there is hardly room to posit any incompatibility between scientific advancement and Christianity. Many scholars would go even further, arguing that the Christian worldview played a significant role in nurturing the development of modern science:

> Their belief in God gave them confidence that the physical world, in all its complexity and vast extent, could be understood.... As a matter of historical fact, modern science has developed from an understanding of the world as God's ordered Creation, with its own inherent rationality.[5]

The great twentieth-century philosopher Alfred North Whitehead made similar arguments. He saw the seeds of modern science in the "medieval insistence on the rationality of God." Confident that the world was the product of a single rational mind, the earlier pioneers of science—all of them Christians—were imbued with an intuition that the world was orderly and lawful.[6]

This is not to say that modern science would never have developed without the aid of religious faith, although there is lively debate on that. However, if the religious belief deeply woven into the European worldview functioned as a framework nurturing the birth of science, then the burden of proof is certainly on those who would claim that religion retarded the growth of science.

Furthermore, religion has not only served to advance scientific discovery, but it also exerts a significant influence on the practical application of scientific discoveries. With the constant advance of technology and medicine—providing drugs that alter the personalities of troubled mental patients, techniques to address issues related to reproduction, new weapons and eavesdropping techniques and so on—new questions are continually raised as to what applications should be deemed ethically acceptable.[7] The scientific method alone does not provide a way of answering these ethical questions but can only help in mapping out the possible alternatives. Such ethical concerns are addressed more naturally from the perspective of religion.

Can Science Inform Religion in Helpful Ways?

As mentioned earlier the Galileo affair is the most well known historic example of the interaction between science and religion. Although often cited as an example of conflict between science and religion, it is also a prime example of scientific contribution to religious belief. In Galileo's time there was a heated disagreement over the interpretation of a few Bible verses in the Psalms. If it was assumed that these Scriptures should be read as modern science, and not as ancient science or perhaps poetry, then they could be interpreted to say that the earth was stationary. However,

Galileo had been convinced by Copernicus's argument that this was impossible, and Galileo wanted to rescue his fellow Christians from this error. Galileo's task was thus to use the new science of his day to *remove a misunderstanding* about what the Bible was teaching about the motion of the earth.

Galileo, who remained a loyal Catholic to the end of his life, makes his position clear in a letter to the Grand Duchess of Tuscany:

> [In] St. Augustine we read: "If anyone shall set the authority of Holy Writ against clear and manifest reason, he who does this knows not what he has undertaken; for he opposes to the truth not the meaning of the Bible, which is beyond his comprehension, but rather his own interpretation, not what is in the Bible, but what he has found in himself and imagines to be there."
>
> This granted, and it being true that two truths cannot contradict one another, it is the function of expositors to seek out the true senses of scriptural texts. These will unquestionably accord with the physical conclusions which manifest sense and necessary demonstrations have previously made certain to us.[8]

Galileo did not suggest that his discoveries *contradicted* the Bible, but that science had offered a refinement to a proper understanding. Projects like this book are motivated by the belief that we need similar guidance today, particularly when interpreting the first chapters of Genesis.

Donald MacKay offers a healthy perspective on scientific involvement with religion:

> Obviously a surface meaning of many passages could be tested, for example, against archaeological discoveries, and the meaning of others can be enriched by scientific and historical knowledge. But I want to suggest that the primary function of scientific enquiry in such fields is neither to verify nor to add to the inspired picture, but to help us in eliminating improper ways of reading it. To pursue the metaphor, I think the scientific data God gives us can sometimes serve as his way of warning us when we are standing too close to the picture, at the wrong angle, or with the wrong expectations, to be able to see the inspired pattern he means it to convey to us.[9]

We suggest that Darwin's theory of evolution, now that it has been confirmed beyond a reasonable doubt by science, offers the same sort of help in understanding the Genesis creation story as Galileo's work helped his generation to better understand the psalmist's references to the mobility of the earth.[10]

Science and religion relate (and don't relate) in many ways, as we have seen. Certainly being independent of each other is common and should be used as the default position. When it is established that there is indeed meaningful interaction, this can be negative or positive, and even both at the same time.

In the Galileo case we all too often assume that "science won and religion lost," but that is an absurd conclusion, especially as Galileo was speaking for an influential group of Catholic astronomers working to reform *their* Church. The conflict was between two different groups within the Catholic Church. Culturally, however, the Church lost in the sense that it was embarrassed and held up to ridicule for its decision, unfairly in the opinion of many scholars. But the Church won in the sense that Galileo's position was eventually validated—by Christian scientists—and the Church moved away from an erroneous interpretation of those Bible verses suggesting that the earth was stationary.[11]

Today, as Christians wrestle with evolution, we see the same dynamics. Many Christians are ridiculed by the secular world and by the more scientifically educated wing of Christianity because of their opposition to Darwin. Many insist on a particular literalist interpretation of a few Bible verses that is not actually consistent with the original Hebrew and close their minds to evolution.[12] This, of course, is a highly negative interaction. But at the same time, as the evidence for evolution becomes ever more compelling, many Christians are embracing alternative interpretations of Genesis and moving away from error.

Although science and religion certainly overlap in some cases, neither is an exhaustive source of truth capable of swallowing up the other. There are still questions that only science can address, and religion should simply concede on those points. And science cannot answer questions about life's purpose or the existence of God. Scientists in the public square should refrain from pontificating on these topics as if suddenly science has become a religion. We also have to keep in mind that science makes mistakes—sometimes significant ones—but science is self-correcting over time, as history shows so clearly.

The historical lesson to be learned here is that Christians should be wary of using the Bible as a scientific text. Every generation has had pundits insisting that the science of its time was taught by the Bible. So Christians confidently wedded their faith to their science only to have it experience a painful divorce when science moved on to new ideas. The faith of many Christians today is wedded to the pre-Darwinian and even pre-geologic science of the nineteenth century, and that marriage is now in serious trouble.

The task of developing dramatic new understandings of Scripture in response to the advance of science is a most challenging undertaking and cannot be taken lightly.

How Do We Know When We Can Adopt a New Understanding of Scripture?

Interpreting Scripture is daunting. C.S. Lewis, who was a respected literary scholar as well as a popular author, advises, "The first demand any work of any art makes upon us is surrender. Look. Listen. Receive."[13] Understanding the Bible is a process of discovery that goes beyond a hasty read through of a translation in modern English. We must study and seek the authors' intended meaning(s) without projecting our own meaning(s) onto the text. This task is known as hermeneutics and is an important part of understanding almost everything.

To read Scripture responsibly, we must note the lessons of history and use what Ernest Lucas calls the "standard methods of biblical interpretation that have been well established since the time of Augustine and the early church fathers."[14] Lucas, with doctorates in biochemistry and theology, explains that these methods involve asking five questions: What kind of language is being used? What kind of literature is it? What is the expected audience? What is the purpose of the text? What relevant extra-textual knowledge is there?[15]

Galileo's seventeenth-century letter to the Grand Duchess addresses these questions, making particular use of knowledge and arguments from outside the Bible that pointed toward a moving earth. In what follows we will look at each of these issues, using some scriptural passages unrelated to the origins controversy to make the point that this approach is essential for dealing with all the Bible and not just the parts that connect to the controversy over evolution.

What Kind of Language Is Being Used?

To understand literature we must first determine the kind of language being used. In the context of biblical interpretation we need to know whether a passage is written in a figurative, symbolic, historical, scientific or straightforward manner. In engaging this task, however, we need to avoid a common error: readers tend to develop *patterns of interpretation* based on the predominant type of text they read. Historians tend to read texts historically, scientists read them scientifically and literary scholars read them as literature. When reading Scripture, understanding the language of a passage may not be intuitive and may require the assistance of scholarly works and commentaries by appropriate experts.

For example, consider the following familiar but confusing statement of Jesus:

> Again I tell you, it is easier for a camel to go through the eye of a needle than for a rich man to enter the kingdom of God. (Matthew 19:24; Mark 10:25; Luke 18:25)

Here, Jesus employs language in a common, literary and entirely legitimate style known as *hyperbole.* When we say we are "so tired we could sleep for a week" or "his mind runs at the speed of light," we are employing hyperbole and have no reason to expect that our listeners will think we are lying because what we say is not literally true. The hyperbolic metaphor that Jesus is using in this passage *could* be taken literally to mean it is impossible for a rich man to enter heaven, but the larger teaching of the Bible would argue against this inference. Furthermore, Jesus shortly thereafter states: "With man this is impossible, but with God all things are possible" (Matthew 19:26; Mark 10:27; Luke 18:27).

Thus, it seems likely that Jesus' first statement is meant to be taken hyperbolically, not literally.

Unfortunately, the surrounding verses—the *context* —are not always so helpful in revealing the language being used. In this case some biblical literalists are uncomfortable with Jesus speaking in hyperbole. They argue that the "eye of the needle" refers literally to a gate in Jerusalem called the "Eye of the Needle." This gate supposedly required a camel to get on its knees to pass through—an act both physically difficult and symbolically humbling. Biblical scholars, however, have shown that there is no historical evidence to support this claim.[16] Others have suggested that the verse is not hyperbole, proposing that there was confusion in the translation between the words for camel and rope.[17] However, a close look at early manuscripts finds the correct word for camel, not rope. Only the more recent translations read rope; the original text thus forces us to conclude that Jesus was speaking hyperbolically in this passage.[18]

As this example shows, the essential task of seeking scholarly insight brings about a fuller appreciation of a passage.

What Kind of Literature Is It?

Literary genre is also important, although we hasten to point out that our modern classification scheme certainly did not exist at the time that the Bible was created. Some of the Scriptures developed originally as an oral tradition centuries before writing even existed; such passages—including the creation accounts in Genesis—contain literary elements designed to make them easier to memorize, such as parallel structures, numerical devices, rhyming and alliteration. Such devices, all but invisible in English translations of the Bible, offer important clues to the nature and meaning of the text.

Setting aside such difficulties it remains the case that scriptural passages inevitably provide clues about their literary type. Just as we have need for completely different types of literature—from legal contracts to scientific papers to heroic poems to novels based on current concerns, like terrorism or global warming—so it was in ancient biblical cultures.

Just as discerning the type of language used in individual phrases, sentences and passages is essential, we must also ask whether the text as a whole is best approached as figurative, historic, scientific or theological. Is this a song, poem, letter or first-person narrative? The literary genres in the

Bible can be categorized as historical narrative (e.g., Kings, Acts), dramatic epic (e.g., Job), law (e.g., Deuteronomy), poetry (e.g., Psalms), wise sayings (e.g., Proverbs), Gospel accounts (e.g., Luke), and apocalyptic writings (e.g., Daniel, Revelation).[19] Literary genres have specific conventions for interpretation, making it essential to determine the literary form before seeking the message of the passage.

Many Christians make the mistake of approaching the Bible as if it were one book with all the implied unity that most books have: one author, one language, one culture, one time period, one audience. We must understand that the Bible is a substantial and wide-ranging *collection* of writings and transcribed oral traditions. John Polkinghorne recommends viewing the Bible as a library rather than a single book. Such an approach would encourage more responsible reading and preclude, for example, the habit of "quote-mining" where isolated passages from different books are combined to draw a conclusion that the texts simply cannot justify.[20]

Who Is the Expected Audience?

The Bible did not drop out of the sky onto the main streets of America with a message written in English aimed at the local residents, analogous to the pamphlets the Allies dropped from the sky onto Germany during the Second World War. The biblical authors did not have us in mind when they wrote

Scripture. We must therefore inquire into the nature of the communications we encounter in the Bible.

Cultural norms, symbolism, the audience's familiarity with existing Scripture and other writings and traditions all contribute to the way that Scripture was written and understood by its original authors and audiences. To take one interesting example, biblical scholars have noted that the ages of the patriarchs in the Old Testament likely had greater symbolic significance to the ancient Hebrews than many currently appreciate.[21] The ages are all multiples of five with seven or fourteen added occasionally, suggesting a symbolic meaning. This strongly suggests that these are not the actual ages of the patriarchs but are rather literary devices that communicated culturally specific information to the intended audience.

Many Christians, perhaps including those reading this page right now, are deeply concerned about such claims, fearing that falsehoods are being attributed to Scripture. Such uneasiness, however, can be assuaged by employing appropriate principles of hermeneutics. We use literary devices all the time today without difficulty. Great achievements are often called "home runs" even if the achiever has never played baseball or is in a wheelchair. A stingy person might be called a "Scrooge" even if his name is Fred. A mute author might be described as speaking with a "powerful voice." Such literary devices occasion no distress when we encounter them in our culture; we should not get agitated when we find ancient cultures using analogous devices in their writings. For reasons that are hard for us to understand today, the importance of figures in the Bible was often expressed by doing interesting things with their ages. No doubt biblical authors would be similarly puzzled by some of our literary conventions today.

Cultural context not only illuminates the *meaning* but it can greatly enrich and enlarge the *message.* Consider the story of the prodigal son described in Luke. A straightforward reading of the parable teaches us about the love and forgiveness of a father toward his son, and consequently about God's love toward his children. However, when the story is considered in its cultural framework, the reading is more profound.

In the local culture the Jewish prodigal son not only acted disgracefully by asking for his inheritance, but he further debased himself by squandering it. The son's behavior warranted a *Kezazah,* or "cutting-off ceremony," on his return. This ceremony would have included rejection by the village and an angry confrontation by his father. The son would have also had to beg for permission to train for a job in the next village. Instead of this harsh and inhospitable reception, a loving and merciful—and culturally exceptional—homecoming awaited the son. As soon as the father saw his son returning, he raced to see him. This is a significant detail since men of the father's age and distinction in the Middle Eastern culture always walked in a slow, dignified manner. By running, the father took on the shame and humiliation due his prodigal son. He then kissed his son, gave him his best robe and called to have the fatted calf slaughtered for a feast—all culturally inappropriate responses likely to be missed by English readers unfamiliar with such customs.

When Jesus originally told this story to a Middle Eastern audience, they likely would have understood the father's love in a more nuanced and profound way than modern readers would derive from a quick read through. Filtering a story like this through an awareness of the original audience and its culture greatly expands our understanding of the passage and discourages inappropriate interpretations.[22]

What Is the Purpose of the Text?

By examining the literary genre, the language and the expected audience, we gain clues to the purpose of the text. Is it written to teach a new lesson or an old lesson in a new light? Does it state the genealogy of a family, highlighting the most significant characters in culturally idiosyncratic ways? Does it describe the love between a man and a woman through poetry? Does it aim to disturb the complacency of an audience or set commonly held misperceptions straight? Texts can have more than one purpose, of course, but the language, genre and expected audience illuminate why it was written in a certain way.

Our goal in this book lies primarily in understanding the message of the Genesis creation accounts—the focal point of so much of the controversy over evolution. We have used other examples so far to make the point that this approach is not something invented just to deal with the problem of origins. When we approach Genesis we emphasize that we must use exactly those techniques that we would use with any other passage.

Old Testament scholars note that Genesis appears to be a *polemical* text challenging other views its readers would have been familiar with. It contains a powerful *monotheism* intended to contrast with the *polytheism* of the Mesopotamian people the Hebrews lived among.[23] When such comparisons are made, the Genesis text emerges as a surprisingly vigorous, in-your-face challenge to the way the rest of the local tribes understood the world. Readers unfamiliar with these other traditions would miss this important insight.

Considering this cultural context, it is thus probably not accidental that the term *lights* was used to describe the sun and the moon as opposed to the Semitic words for sun and moon, which were also the names of pagan gods. By not using these names, the Genesis account depersonalizes the heavens, essentially claiming that the sun and moon are merely lights in the sky, not deities looking down from on high. By analogy a modern science writer might deliberately insult astrologers by referring to Venus and Mars as the "second and fourth planets," completely disregarding the names of the planets so near and dear to the hearts of those who think the planets shape their lives.

The Genesis text, which originated as an oral tradition centuries before the Hebrews had writing, reveals a stark contrast to the established belief systems that surrounded the Hebrews. This was not the only reason Genesis was written, of course, as it also contains much original content about God, creation, worship and other elements of faith and life. However, understanding this polemical purpose enriches and informs the proper interpretation of Genesis.

What Relevant Extratextual Knowledge Exists?

Beyond the elements of language, audience and the text itself there is often other relevant information that deepens the understanding of a passage. For example, awareness that Paul was writing from jail in some of his New Testament letters may be helpful to put them in context.[24] Knowledge that passages may have originated as oral traditions is also helpful.

Extratextual knowledge is critically important for the process of translation. The biblical languages are not spoken today, so we have to figure out what the words actually mean. This problem is quite serious because biblical Hebrew has very few words compared to English. The entire vocabulary is just over eight thousand words, a fraction of the number of words that must have been used by the Israelites. By way of comparison the second edition of the *Oxford English Dictionary* contains entries for 171,476 words in current use, and 47,156 obsolete words. There are few additional ancient Hebrew texts to use for comparison, as well, so finding the intended meaning is often a great challenge. Biblical Hebrew is written without vowels, which often makes very different words identical. The five English words *bag, beg, big, bog* and *bug* are different and easily distinguished. But without vowels they all look the same, giving us, in print, one "word" with five very different meanings. Many words in the Hebrew sections of the Bible thus permit several different meanings to be assigned to them. In some cases translators encounter words that simply do not appear outside the Bible; about half of the words in the Hebrew Bible occur three times or less; many occur just once. In many cases the same Hebrew word is used in place of several English words. Determining the best English meaning of such words is thus incredibly difficult. We must therefore exercise extreme caution before we insist that a certain English passage in the Bible has to be interpreted in a particular way.

This problem arises in the first verse of the Bible: "In the beginning God created the heavens *[shamay-im]* and the earth *[)erets]*." When we convert the letters for the Hebrew word for "heavens" to our alphabet—a process called transliteration—we get *shamayim,* which also means "sky," which the translators used, for example, in Genesis 1:9 ("Let the water under the *sky [shamayim]* be gathered to one place"). *Shamayim* also means "air," which was the English word used in 1 Samuel 17:44 and 1 Kings 16:4.

The Hebrew word translated "earth" in the first verse of the Bible is *erets* which also means "land," the choice of translators in Deuteronomy 1:27 ("You grumbled in your tents and said, 'Because the Lord hates us; He has brought us out of the land *[erets]* of Egypt'"). The Genesis account could thus have begun, "In the beginning God created the *land* and the *sky.*" This, in fact, would actually be much closer to how the ancient Hebrews would have interpreted it. They had no need for an additional, specific word to refer to "planet earth" since they had no concept of a planet. Likewise, they had no concept of the "heavens" beyond the sky. Their entire universe was the land, which they thought extended to the waters on all sides, and a solid dome-like sky overhead, to which the stars were fixed, and above which were storehouses of rain and snow. Neither the writer of this verse nor his audience had any concept of a planet called "earth" suspended in the midst of the heavens, surrounded by a vast array of stars and galaxies. To suppose that) *erets* in Genesis refers to the *planet* earth is to assign to that Hebrew word a meaning that neither the writer nor his audience could possibly have comprehended. To assign it this meaning is to violate almost every canon of interpretation.[25]

This insight would have been helpful to biblical scholars at the time of Galileo. Instead of worrying that the psalmist had written "The world is firmly established; it cannot be moved," they could have understood that the psalmist was referring to the land under his feet—which is solid with respect to the people who stand on it—not the globe suspended in space that moves around the sun.

Extratextual knowledge is indispensable to both *translating* and *understanding* the biblical texts. The advance of our knowledge in science, history and linguistics provides ongoing insights that help us interpret texts in light of relevant discoveries.

How Does This Approach Help with Genesis?

Considering how a Scripture passage fits into the context of the greater Bible story is especially important. In addition to asking the five questions listed earlier, the reader should ask how the passage fits in with the rest of the Bible. More specifically, how do the themes in the passage relate to what the Bible reveals about the character of God, the nature of human beings and the person of Jesus? How do successive writings make use of earlier writings? Taking this approach, it is evident that Genesis 1–11 presents themes of sin and grace that continue throughout the Bible and into the New Testament.[26]

Readers have interpreted the Genesis creation story in various ways over the centuries. The literalist reading of Genesis 1–2 that is so common today differs greatly from the interpretation of earlier church leaders including Origen, Augustine and Aquinas. Christian theologians have been open to the idea of a nonliteralist interpretation of Genesis 1–2 since long before evolutionary theory existed.

We emphasize that the opening chapters of Genesis contain signs warning against literalist interpretations. There are *two* stories of creation, not one, and they differ in important details. These different accounts push readers to be open to truths that run deeper than merely historical accounts, and to be wary of interpreting every word in a scientifically literal way. In the first creation account, God creates the plants, marine animals, birds, land animals, and then man and woman together (Genesis 1:1– 2:3). In the second account, however, God creates man first and then plants, land animals and birds, and finally woman from Adam's rib (Genesis 2:4-25). Clearly, the order of creation differs in these accounts, and only an unreasonable interpretation that mutilates the text can resolve the differences. "Discrepancies" like this suggest that these passages were never understood as we understand modern history today. They simply must be read through different lenses.

We make progress when we set aside demands that Genesis 1 and 2 be treated as parallel modern historical accounts that, by the canons of today's scholarship, must agree in every detail, like the accounts of a crime provided by two different witnesses. If we ask, instead, about the *theological* meaning, we find no disagreement. These passages tell us who God is, what the world is, and what it means to be human. They reveal God's desire to be in relationship with the creation. Through these passages we know that God transcends but interacts with the world. And we know the universe was not created through a cosmic battle among squabbling deities, as claimed by other creation myths of the day. God is not an abstract concept but a personal being; his Spirit hovers over the waters (Genesis 1:2) in loving concern for the activities of the creation. God is an artist bringing beauty from ugliness and order from disorder. The world is a place of order, open to discovery and exploration; a place of diversity and beauty, the world is good (Genesis 1:31). The pinnacle of that goodness is humankind, made in God's image and charged by God to be caretakers of the creation.

Biblical interpretation falls short without an understanding of divine inspiration, of course, and we do not suggest that the Bible is simply another book to be interpreted. But we do a great disservice to the concept and power of inspiration when we reduce it to mere factual accuracy, as though God's role were nothing more than a divine fact checker, preventing the biblical authors from making mistakes. A dead and lifeless text, like the phone book, can be factually accurate. The inspiration of the Bible is dynamic and emerges through engagement with readers.

The Bible is thus both literature and more than literature; it functions for many readers as a powerful meditation drawing them into the presence of God. Bible reading is thus often accompanied by prayer; this opens the conversation with God to receive the message with the proper state of mind and spirit.

When we read the Bible, we join our hearts and minds with literally billions of Christians across centuries and continents and cultures in a common experience that has defined Christian worship since the first century. We know in time to come that billions more Christians will read the Bible. We are a part of that tradition, informed by the wisdom of the past that passes through our experience and into the future. We must always be mindful of this rich, living tradition and not cut ourselves off from it as though we live in a unique time with privileged insights that need not be informed by those who have gone before. In humility we must also recognize that we are certainly not immune to correction by those who come after.

4

Can Scientific and Scriptural Truth Be Reconciled?

You will know the truth, and the truth will set you free.

JOHN 8:32

Once upon a time, truth was a simple concept. There was a world "out there," and when we made statements about the world that matched its reality, then those statements were considered true. This commonsense notion still guides our practical understanding. When we say, "The sun comes up every morning," or "Willie Mays played center field," or "It is colder in the winter than the summer," we state those things as "true facts" because we know the world actually is that way. The sun *does* come up in the morning, Willie Mays *did* play center field, and it *is* colder in the winter. We rarely need to reflect on what it means to believe that those claims are true.

But there are areas where truth becomes more complex. When we list, for example, the "Great

Books of the Western World" and claim "Shakespeare, Dante, Petrarch and Plato are great writers," critics respond that such claims are culturally biased. They are "power grabs" asserted to establish the superiority of Western culture, white males or Europeans with two-syllable names. Such claims are not true in any ultimate sense, but only within a limited cultural perspective with its own idiosyncratic values. Similar problems face religious claims. When we say that "Christianity is true" or that "Protestant Christianity is superior to Roman Catholicism," we are challenged by those who would argue the opposite. And we find ourselves with no simple way to sift truth from error.

Ethical and moral claims are also problematic. What does it mean to say, "Torture is *wrong*"? Can such claims be true? If so, in what sense *are* they true?

Even in science, where truth claims often seem to have a powerful simplicity, the situation has become increasingly complex. While it is true that statements like "Hot air rises" or "Ice melts at 0 degrees centigrade" are indeed simple, there are many scientific statements that are harder to evaluate. Claims about quantum mechanical probabilities, electrical "fields," the existence of multiple universes or life on other planets, the nature of time and so on don't have a simple factual character.

These and other complexities have motivated some scholars to challenge the very notion of truth. Perhaps, they argue, truth is illusory—something with only a local meaning relevant to a particular situation and people with a particular set of assumptions. This is the position taken by many postmodernists. In the so-called modern period, which has supposedly ended, truth was accepted as a realistic and obtainable goal, with scientific truth as the model.

We reject the idea that there is no such thing as truth. In fact, virtually all scientists reject this central claim of postmodernity, and to the degree they think about it at all, most scientists continue to function as though there has been no transition from modernity to postmodernity. We would argue that well-tested scientific claims about the world, like Einstein's famous relationship between mass and energy, $E=mc^2$, are true without qualification, not "local" in any sense and certainly not embedded in some cultural context. All physicists believe that this basic truth about the physical universe is also true in other galaxies, and although they would write it differently, alien physicists would also have discovered it.

While it might seem a minor point to assert that basic scientific claims about the world are true, the reality is that acceptance of this simple fact refutes the sweeping claim of the postmodernist that truth does not exist. And, having established that truth can indeed be discovered by humans, we are then free to pursue truth in a more general sense, seeking it out in other areas, like theology and ethics, and confident that the search is reasonable.

In this chapter we explore ways that the truths of science, theology and Scripture come into contact with each other, and how to deal with apparent conflicts.

What Do We Do When Science Seems to Conflict with Scripture?

Through the development and advance of science we continually discover more about the universe. Such discoveries lead to an increasing accumulation of scientific truth. For believers these discoveries must ultimately be compatible with the truth revealed in the Bible, and it is our conviction that this compatibility is both desirable and possible. The limitation, as the postmodernists hasten to remind us, is that our access to all forms of truth, including scientific and religious truth, is at best partial and always compromised by our cultural, personal and intellectual limitations.

The Bible is not a scientific text and should not be read that way. Science did not even exist five hundred years ago, and scientific literature is a recent and highly specialized form of communication. Reading the Bible as a scientific text, while it may seem natural, overlooks the significance of the fact that the biblical authors were real human beings who lived in certain times and places, spoke certain languages and had their own worldviews. And they all lived before there even was science. We disrespect Moses, David, Paul and even Jesus when we assume they communicate by our rules today. We must allow them to be authentic members of their own time and then make the effort to understand what that means.

Making the biblical authors into modern, scientifically literate thinkers and writers immediately produces inconsistencies between the Bible and the scientifically determined history of the world. However, when Scripture is read in context, these inconsistencies disappear. We can therefore safely accept Scripture as God's revealed Word, even though it does not address the specifics of many scientific questions and often refers to the natural world using the understandings of the time in which it was written.

The first step in addressing apparent conflicts between science and religion is the recognition that they are different enterprises. These differences are often highlighted by noting that science and religion answer different questions or answer the same question in different ways.

John Polkinghorne, the world's leading scholar of the science-religion interface, has developed a winsome analogy to illustrate this point. He asks, "Why is the water in the tea kettle boiling?" And he notes that there is more than one answer to that question.[1] The scientific answer might be because the burning gas under the kettle heats the water. Another acceptable though very different and nonscientific answer could be that the water is boiling because I want to make a cup of tea.[2] Both of these answers are true, of course, and both accurately describe the reason for the boiling water, although from different perspectives. The latter response addresses the question of purpose that, for most people, is the most important part of any explanation.

The kinds of answers found in the Scriptures are generally *nonscientific,* but not because the Bible is teaching an ancient science that has been overturned. They are nonscientific because the Bible is not even trying to teach science. Nowhere in the entire Bible do we read anything that even hints that the writer is trying to teach science. What we encounter instead is a consistent discussion of the purposes and reasons for why things are the way they are.

This is not to say the Bible *lacks* historical, objective or scientific truth. For example, the Bible reports the existence of the Christmas star, and science offers a possible explanation for the star's origin.[3] The resurrection of Jesus is another example where the Bible is not limited to giving an explanation of why something happened, but also makes a statement about an event in history. The Bible speaks of rain falling and rainbows appearing in the sky. But in all these cases it is crystal clear that the writers are focusing on the meaning of the events, not the history or science relevant to understanding them.

Polkinghorne sums up this relationship between science and religion:

> Neither [science nor religion] attains exhaustive knowledge—for the exploration of nature continually reveals new and unexpected insights, and the infinite reality of God will always exceed the grasp of finite human beings—but both [science and religion] believe that they achieve verisimilitude, the making of maps of aspects of reality that are adequate for some, but not every, purpose.[4]

Science will never fully answer the why questions of religion; science can tell us only how the world *is*—never the reasons or purposes for why it is that way. Moreover, a complete understanding of the mysteries of our existence will probably never be developed by the finite human mind anyway, so there will always be bona fide science questions that science cannot answer. We may never know, to take a simple example, what happened before the big bang or even if there was a "before."

Finally, we note that it requires a certain level of faith to answer the scientific questions of how something happens. Answers to scientific questions assume that the laws of the universe are constant or, if recent speculations turn out to be true, the laws are changing in only the most subtle of ways.[5] This requires faith in the orderliness of nature. With or without belief in an ultimate Creator, we must have faith that this universal order is real, reliable and accessible to the limited powers of our minds. Without such a belief, science could not give an explanation for anything.

But Doesn't Science Constantly Change Its Explanations for Natural Phenomena?

Error is intrinsic to all human activity, including science; our technology is also imperfect and not capable of measuring anything with absolute precision; and human comprehension is incomplete and sometimes compromised by personal issues. All these factors contribute to a limited understanding of even the clearest scientific truths.

Sometimes people who do not like certain scientific ideas, like evolution or the big bang, will reject them on the basis that "science is always changing" and, in essence, hold out hope that the scientific community will soon converge on some new set of ideas more to their liking. We caution against this hope, for although science has historically experienced some revolutionary changes, most of its central ideas, once established, are not *changed* but merely *refined.*

For example, Copernicus suggested in 1543 that the earth was going around the sun in a perfect circle. This idea was refined a half-century later when Kepler said the orbit was not quite a circle but an ellipse. Many people during this time were upset at the idea that the earth was not the center of the universe, but they were hardly relieved when Kepler corrected Copernicus only by changing the shape of the orbits ever so slightly.

A century later geologists became convinced that the earth was much older than the so-called biblical chronologies, which placed its age at under ten thousand years based on literalist readings of the Old Testament chronologies, could accommodate. One of the first such "scientific" ages for the earth was that of the French naturalist Georges-Louis Leclerc, Comte de Buffon (1707-1788), who estimated the age of the earth at around seventy-five thousand years. A few decades after Buffon, the physicist Lord Kelvin estimated the age of the earth at 100 million years. And now virtually all scientists agree that the earth is around 4.5 billion years old, a number that has not changed for some time, despite a great amount of progress in making such measurements. Whatever frustrations attended the demise of the biblically based estimates for the age of the earth in the eighteenth century have certainly not diminished since then. Quite the opposite, as the measured age has migrated with ever more confidence even further from the desired number.

So, while science certainly discovers new things that sometimes refute old things, the reality is that science is self-correcting. Scientific findings, especially now that science has become such a central part of our modern civilization, are constantly tested, updated and peer reviewed. Inaccuracies are corrected when new discoveries and experiments bring the truth to light more fully. This does not mean that the truth has changed, of course. Rather, the tools used to find the truth revealed their limitations due to the state of the technology, inadequate understanding or misinterpretation of data. As these tools improve, science leads us closer and closer to the truth.

A helpful analogy is to think about the development of scientific theories as *map making.* A map gathers different kinds of data, like longitude and latitude, elevations and waterways, to make a coherent representation of reality. The map, of course, is not reality itself but a *model* of reality. Scientific "maps" of reality, known as theories, need updating in response to new discoveries or improved understanding. But just as new maps are essentially refinements rather than refutations of old maps, so most new scientific theories are rarely refutations of their predecessors.

Selfish motivations and scientific errors, of course, play a role in scientific discovery. Self-promoting individuals sometimes push for outcomes that advance their reputation. A desire for particular results or an assumption about the ways things are can result in manipulation of data, whether consciously or unconsciously. And there have been some significant examples of such contrived data in the history of science.

One chronicle of how such distortions were perpetuated can be found in Stephen Jay Gould's *The Mismeasure of Man,* which tells the tragic story of how nineteenth-century scientists found alleged data to support prevailing prejudices about the relationship between race and intelligence.[6] Another example occurred when paleontologists, eagerly looking for "missing links" on the human family tree, were duped into thinking that "Piltdown Man" was an actual pre-human fossil when, in fact, it was a joke.[7] What we must not forget, however, is that these errors were uncovered and corrected by the ongoing practice of science. No referee from outside science had to come in and point out the error. The historical record is abundantly clear that the scientific community does a good job of correcting its own errors and moving steadily forward toward a better understanding of reality.

The scientific method standardizes and minimizes the bias and prejudice of an experimenter. The greatest tool in this method is the necessity of *repeatability*. If a startling new discovery is made in a lab in New York, bringing fame to the scientists in charge, they had better hope that their counterparts in Tokyo measure exactly the same thing when they do the experiment.

There are, however, certain types of errors that are not so easily eliminated, and those are the random errors associated with all measuring instruments. No scientific experiment is exactly precise, and error must always be considered. But the presence of these errors, which are generally quite small, is rarely license to reject the claims being made about the world.

The imperfections of humans and their methods means that scientific conclusions will never be perfect, but they will certainly improve with time as scientific advances continue to self-correct. Although such critiques and qualifications of the veracity of science are important to consider, we must not let them blind us to the enormous successes of science in uncovering the patterns of nature.

Can We Ever Know Anything With Absolute Certainty?

Human limitations may prevent us from *fully* understanding any parts of our experience, including Scripture, religious experience and science. What we perceive as conflicts, therefore, may actually be misunderstandings that simply require further consideration. Moreover, because God is so far beyond us, there will be pieces—perhaps very large pieces—of the ultimate truth that always remain a mystery, and apparent contradictions that never get resolved. Robert Trigg reflects on the reality of this limited understanding:

> Our reason is, like a candle, pale and flickering, compared with the light of God's wisdom. Nevertheless, it was sufficient to enable us to gain some knowledge. There was plenty of room for error, and partial knowledge, but we were,

> it was thought, made in the image of God, and could obtain a glimmer of understanding through science, and other operations of the human mind.[8]

This concept is also found in the slogan of the Cambridge Platonists, a school of theologians and philosophers influential at the time of the founding of Britain's Royal Society in 1660: "Reason is the candle of the Lord."[9]

Francis Bacon, the great champion of the strength of scientific induction, observes:

> To conclude, therefore, let no man upon a weak conceit of sobriety or an ill-applied moderation think or maintain that a man can search too far, or be too well studied in the book of God's word, or the book of God's works, divinity or philosophy; but rather let men endeavor an endless progress or proficiency in both; only let men beware that they apply both to charity, and not to swelling; to use, and not to ostentation; and again, that they do not unwisely mingle or confound these learnings together.[10]

We now have some useful tools to guide us in our exploration of some key ideas where science comes into contact with religion. We have established that the Bible is not a textbook of science and can only be properly understood when we consider it in its historical and cultural context. And science, while always advancing, is actually not so much *changing* as it is *improving.* Our task, then, begins with the recognition that we should assume that well-established mainstream scientific ideas are reliable and that the contextual understanding of the Bible provides the best guide to its meaning.

What Role Could God Have in Evolution?

The broadest and most general question we are addressing in this book is how to understand evolution as the way that God created life. This question, in fact, is the basis for this entire book.

The claim that evolution accounts for the diversity of present life forms seems to imply to many people that God played no role in the process of evolution. If this is true, it clearly contradicts a central doctrine of creation for many faiths. Christianity professes a God actively involved in creation. Many faiths share this concept of an interactive God, a belief known as *theism.* Belief in an uninvolved, disinterested God who created "in the beginning" is *deism.* Understanding the interaction of God with the created order is the problem of divine action or *providence.*

Divine action figured prominently in discussions of Darwin's theory in the late nineteenth century. For some theologians evolution was compatible with theism only if God acted supernaturally at points in the evolutionary process.[11] For example, some suggested that while animals and plants evolved, maybe God created Adam and Eve supernaturally rather than through a more gradual, natural development. Other theologians saw the uninterrupted process of evolution as compatible with Christian doctrine, understanding evolution to be "the silent and regular working of him who, in the fullness of time, utters his voice in Christ and the cross."[12] But while most theologians—and scientists, for that matter—were comfortable with evolution, most of them supplemented Darwin's theory of natural selection with other processes like divine intervention or built-in teleological trajectories that unfolded God's preordained creative intent.

We still passionately share the desire to understand God's involvement in the world, one of the central ideas at the heart of the science-and-religion conversation. We affirm that God can act outside the created physical laws, but we do not say that miraculous events *outside* the laws of nature are the *only* instances of God's involvement. We want to argue most insistently that God's creative work can be done *through* the laws of nature, and not merely by *breaking* or *suspending* those laws.

There is a powerful analogy here with the incarnation. God's purposes in Jesus were accomplished by actually becoming a human and embracing all the limitations that came with that. In Jesus we see God actually entering into the natural order and taking the form of one of its creatures.

This is a powerful and deep truth, mysterious certainly, but at the heart of Christianity. We want to suggest, by analogy, that God's creative purposes can be similarly realized by being incarnate in natural history. Just as Jesus did not have to be continuously "supplemented" by supernatural interventions, so the ongoing creative processes in nature that gave rise to the diversity of life do not need to be continually supplemented.

The model for divinely guided evolution that we are proposing here thus requires no "intrusions from outside" for its account of God's creative process, except for the origins of the natural laws guiding the process. We do not rule these out, of course, nor claim they are not possible. Rather, we suggest that "once life arose, the process of evolution and natural selection permitted the development of biological diversity and complexity," and "humans are part of this process." Moreover, "once evolution got under way, no special supernatural intervention was required."[13]

And, without apology, we are happy to acknowledge that we hold this position because it is most consistent with what science has discovered about the world.

So how are these ideas reconciled with a theistic, interactive God instead of the disinterested God of deism? Is it rational to believe that God was involved in the Darwinian history of the world?

Where Does God Fit in the Grand Explanation?

Before considering what room exists for divine action in nature, we must clarify how far this idea should be taken. In searching for an understanding of God's involvement in the unfolding course of events, we do not suggest that God is directly responsible for every single event in cosmic history. If that were the case, then God would be responsible for every human thought, every event and even every natural disaster. Such a concept of God challenges the reality of free will and makes the creation nothing more than a self-indulgent exercise on God's part.

We suggest instead that a proper understanding of theism affirms that God has endowed nature with a degree of freedom. In much the same way that humans can act freely in the world without coercion from God, so nature itself has an inherent liberty. This is not to say that nature has a mind of its own, but only that the unfolding patterns of nature are not restricted to machinelike, predetermined paths. Polkinghorne explains:

> [There] is no doubt that part of God's interaction with the world must be that of letting agents or circumstances take their course. Without that there would be no true freedom, and the gift of love in creation must be the gift of freedom, both to humankind and also to the Universe itself, as

> it explores its own inherent potential through its evolving process.[14]

Our view, in agreement with Christian thinkers across the centuries and many thoughtful theologians today, rejects the concept of a God who is involved in the creation at certain times and only observes at other times. In harmony with the most generally accepted concept of theism, we affirm a God who is at *all* times involved, yet who still allows a degree of freedom to the creation.

Are the Laws of Nature Free?

Well before Darwin's contribution to biology, the scientific revolution in physics, largely through the work of Isaac Newton, marked a tremendous advance in our understanding of the physical world. Scientists discovered that the world's behavior could be explained and predicted with great accuracy on the basis of physical laws. Nature, as understood at the time, appeared to reliably follow a set of fundamental rules. The motion of planets, for example, could be explained as a necessary result of their obedience to gravity. This understanding of the world supported the traditional belief in a rational, consistent Creator.

But, as Polkinghorne puts it, these laws might also come across as "a gift from the Greeks."[15] Given a second look, they appear to challenge basic theism. For as much as these laws signify a rational Creator, their trustworthiness could also imply God's absence. Centuries before Newton some Christians believed that angels pushed the planets around in their orbits. Now these angels were no longer needed, replaced by Newton's new laws of motion. When natural phenomena are explained by the laws of nature, is there still a role for God, other than as the Sustainer of those laws?

In the wake of Newton's work, Christians found it increasingly hard to understand how God could take an active role in the universe without upsetting the natural course of events. Furthermore, the natural phenomena explained by Newton seemed to be entirely deterministic, with no flexibility or wiggle room of any sort. The world seemed to be without any inherent freedom, which posed questions about human freedom as well. Freedom could only exist in a world where the laws of nature were somehow open or flexible. The world's future cannot be entirely determined or predictable from any given moment if there is to be true freedom. These concerns, to say the least, were unsettling.

Fortunately, the mechanical worldview of Newton and the scientific revolution is now a relic of the past. Modern physics has replaced it with a radically different picture of the world, thanks to quantum mechanical uncertainty and some ideas misnamed "chaos" theory.

Quantum uncertainty, as understood by most physicists, reveals that the world of the very small—like the electrons—is not determined. Electrons, to a surprising degree, "do their own thing" and do not rigorously follow paths determined by any laws, in dramatic contrast to planets. Any phenomena dependent on the behavior of electrons will have a tiny degree of unpredictability and will appear, in an odd way, to be "free."

Chaos, or the "chaotic unpredictability of complex systems," reveals that certain phenomena, like the weather, depend on immeasurably small inputs of initial energy in such a way that they simply cannot be predicted, because we cannot know the initial conditions accurately enough. The classic example is the so-called butterfly effect, in which a butterfly flapping its wings in New York creates a hurricane in Tokyo. As odd as it sounds, phenomena exactly like this have been observed in nature.

Chaos and quantum uncertainty make it impossible to see the world any longer as determined. The future no longer appears to be the simple extrapolation of the present, and complete knowledge of the present would not be enough to predict the future. The world now seems free in ways that seem similar to how we are free.

A complete and detailed explanation of nature's behavior simply cannot be provided any longer, which is exactly the opposite of how the world looked in the wake of the scientific revolution. Newtonian mechanics clearly implied that science could in principle eventually provide a complete explanation of any and perhaps even all natural events. Now, though, we understand that the laws of nature are such that scientific prediction and explanation are ultimately limited. These limitations do not create an "anything goes" universe, of course. The moon cannot suddenly reverse direction or hop over to Mars and orbit that planet for a while. Rain cannot fall up, nor ice sink instead of float. But within the crannies of this orderly world, tiny bits of freedom lurk.

It is thus perfectly possible that God might influence the creation in subtle ways that are unrecognizable to scientific observation. In this way modern science opens the door to divine action without the need for law-breaking miracles. Given the impossibility of absolute prediction or explanation, the laws of nature no longer preclude God's action in the world. Our perception of the world opens once again to the possibility of divine interaction.

God's interaction with the world is deeply mysterious, of course, and nobody has ever produced any sort of picture for how we might think about this. But we hasten to point out—and this is very significant—we also do not understand *human* action in the world. We make plans every day: we choose clothes to wear, food for breakfast, a route to work and the first task of the day. These human intentions emerge in our minds, somehow, via processes that we don't understand. And then we rearrange the world around us to make these intentions a reality; we make things happen that would not otherwise occur, but we do this without "breaking the laws of nature." Because this process is common, we take it for granted and presume there is nothing deeply mysterious going on. But this is simply not true. The changes we bring about in the world derive from a process that originates in the deep and inaccessible recesses of our minds.

We suggest therefore that God's interaction with the world might be analogous to our own, just more substantial. Christians have always affirmed that God has intentions and that the providential course of history is influenced by God realizing these intentions. We thus suggest that God's interaction with the world, in analogy with ours, need not require that the laws of nature be constantly "broken."

The uncertainty and unpredictability of the world does not force us to reject the earlier understanding of God's creation as consistent and reliable. After all, the world still exhibits the same orderly behavior that inspired so many faithful scientists of earlier centuries. Regardless of the unpredictability of quantum mechanical or complex, chaotic systems, the sun stills rises and sets, the tides ebb and flow, and objects fall to the ground. Nature is reliable enough to reflect God's faithfulness, yet flexible enough to permit God's involvement, just as it is open to our involvement and the involvement of all creatures.

What About God's Relationship to Time?

An important assumption undergirds this discussion: God's action can be compared to our own. We are mindful that this statement might seemed loaded with hubris, but all we mean is that we need to have *something* that we understand, to even *think* about things beyond our understanding. "God talk" has always been deeply metaphorical, especially in the Bible where God is described as Father, Creator, Shepherd, a "still small voice" and so on. To make any statements about God we need to use language with words that have familiar meanings.

In suggesting the possibility of divine action, we tend to assume that God would need the same sort of openings in nature's laws that humans need, as they influence the unfolding course of events. And this is indeed one critically important way to think about this. However, we add that God's action is also profoundly and necessarily different from human action.

For example, God's relationship to time, a deep and enduring theological consideration, greatly affects divine action. If God is creator of the universe as a whole—and if time is a part of this universe—then God's relationship to time is not restricted to only the present moment, as our actions are. We can speculate, for example, that God creates a world where certain free things happen, but happen along channels that have a high degree of predictability. By analogy, the water in the Niagara River definitely goes over the Falls, but we cannot chart its path accurately. Perhaps God creates a world where his foreknowledge allows him to see unfolding channels of history without needing to control or even know certain small details. Or perhaps God knows all the details without actually determining them. We all have foreknowledge of what will happen to a brick if we drop it on our toe, but this foreknowledge hardly causes the brick to fall or the pain to appear.

Because God's perception of time differs from our own, God's action in time may differ in important ways from ours. We cannot understand God's existence outside of time, however, since we have no concepts to help us with that, so we are obviously limited in our understanding of God's action.

Conclusion

We suggest that our modern understanding of physical laws, combined with an appreciation of the complex ways that God probably relates to time, can be synthesized into a robust theistic worldview. Darrel Falk provides the following perspective:

> The Bible tells us that God created, but it does not tell us how, and we need to be careful that we do not force the God of the universe into one of our human molds. We must not limit God's activity to our conceptions of how we think we would work if we were God....

> The Bible states that God gave the creation command and that this resulted in each of the various "kinds" being produced. It is clear that, as a result of God's command and in his Presence, scores of elephantlike species were created, but the Bible does not specify that God uttered a unique command, one at a time, for each new species. Just as God built freedom into the nation of Israel, and just as God builds freedom into our lives today, so freedom may well be a central component of God's biological world as well. This is not to say that God is not playing a supervisory role in creation in a manner resembling the role God plays in my life and yours. But there is no a priori scriptural reason to assume that the biological world was created one species at a time by the God of the Universe "pushing creation buttons" each time he wanted a new species. He does not do that in the daily affairs of my life (for which I am grateful), and there is no reason, scriptural or otherwise, to assume that he does that in the biological world either. God's Spirit guides the progression of life. His Presence is never far from creation, just as it is never far from the events of my life. Nonetheless God respects my freedom and (I suspect) values freedom in the rest of creation as well.[16]

We caution against oversimplifying this topic or even constructing complex and elaborate models for how God interacts with the physical world. These are the deepest imaginable questions, and we must not expect simple answers. The Christian tradition has always affirmed that God *loves,* God *knows* and God *acts,* but we have no "theories" of how God does any of these things. Our goal should be to avoid narrowing down the range of possibilities by putting God in boxes of our own devising. We must also avoid inadvertently presuming that faith plays no role. Many deeply committed Christians are quite comfortable looking at the unfolding patterns of natural history through the eyes of faith and affirming that God's intentions are being realized, even though they have no model for exactly how that is happening. These are not scientific questions, although science does shape the discussion by steering us toward certain options. In the final analysis these will remain matters of faith, which is where they have always been.

5

Science and the Existence of God

The fool says in his heart,

"There is no God."

PSALM 14:1

The existence of God is an enduring and popular philosophical problem that entwines with many aspects of human experience, as we will see in this chapter. Many arguments claiming to prove the existence of God have been proposed throughout the centuries, often on the basis of some feature of the natural world, like its remarkable fine-tuning for life or transcendent moral laws. But there are also more general arguments for the existence of God such as the origin of the world itself—the fact that there is something rather than nothing.

There have also been attempts to *disprove* the existence of God. The world often appears cruel and without meaning, leading some to deny that it was created by a being resembling the God of Christianity. Disproving the existence of God in a general sense is a more complex task, however, for reasons that have to do more with logic than the details of reality.

Consider how much easier it is to establish that there *is* a black swan somewhere on the earth than establishing that there *isn't* one. To *prove* that black swans exist we simply have to produce one. To *disprove* the existence of black swans we have to make a case that we have searched so thoroughly that there simply isn't any possibility that we have overlooked something. G.K. Chesterton, with his usual succinct insight, made this exact point: "Atheism is indeed the most daring of all dogmas.... For it is the assertion of a universal negative."[1]

Popular arguments for the existence of God, many of which predate Christianity, take a variety of forms, some of which interact in interesting ways with the scientific view of the world:

- The *cosmological argument*—dating all the way back to Aristotle in the fourth century B.C.—argues that there must be a first cause (God) to start the global chain of causality.
- The *teleological argument* or *argument from design* argues that the universe has a high degree of complex order that could only have been created by God. Versions of this argument, which was championed by William Paley shortly before Darwin, are promoted enthusiastically today by the intelligent design movement.
- The *ontological argument* is based on a clever but obscure argument about a "being greater than

which none can be conceived." It starts simply with a concept of God. Anselm of Canterbury in the eleventh century and contemporary philosopher Alvin Plantinga formulate this argument to show that if it is logically possible for God (a necessary being) to exist, then God exists. Most people don't find this argument convincing.

- Arguments that nonphysical qualities observed in the universe are genuinely real and not illusory, such as morality, beauty, love or religious experience, are arguments against the possibility that everything can be explained in a purely materialistic way and thus argue for a reality beyond the physical.
- The *transcendental argument* suggests that logic, science, ethics and other things we take seriously do not make sense in the absence of God, and that atheistic arguments must ultimately refute themselves if pressed with rigorous consistency, since they are not based on a logic outside themselves.

Each of these arguments supports a *certain type* of belief in a *certain type* of creator; some of them invoke the characteristics of the natural world, while others are based more on pure logic. The ontological argument has no connection of any sort with the scientific view of the world. None of the arguments are conclusive, but they can at least be juxtaposed against arguments that God does not exist, like the problem of evil, or the absence of certain types of observational evidence for God.

The response of critics to many of these arguments is "If God created the world, what created God?"

How can postulating the existence of God actually explain anything? Are we not simply pushing the question further back? We can hardly explain how an iPhone got to the moon by saying, "It came in that fancy box over there." Such a response simply changes the question to "How did the box get here?" If we want to explain the existence of something as grounded in God, we must justify how God's existence is less puzzling than whatever we are trying to explain.

This requires serious consideration. Arguments for God's existence often seem like little more than logical dominos, which just keep punting the question rather than answering it, like an annoying child repeating *why?* over and over again, as if the answers are not going anywhere. Certainly we must not make the naive assumption that simply saying "God created it" explains anything in the absence of some reason why the existence of God is not itself a problem to be solved.

We will suggest in this chapter that the grand project of proving or disproving the existence of God in any final sense is a project from the past, an exercise for a generation with more confidence in human reason than most of us have today. Nevertheless, the futility of *absolute* proof does not mean that reasons for or against belief in God cannot be meaningfully discussed and even embraced as evidence.

Science intersects with arguments for and against the existence of God in two important places. The most interesting is the problem of the fine-tuning of the universe, to which we devote chapter seven. It is a most satisfying way to close a discussion of the interaction of science and faith. We begin this chapter with a different argument often used *against* the existence of God. This is the argument that the world is so evil and purposeless that there cannot be a creator like the Christian God behind it. Our job will be to undermine this powerful and enduring argument against the existence of God.

Doesn't Evolution Make the Problem of Evil Much Worse?

The problem of evil poses the most ancient and persistent objection to God's existence. Of all the challenges to faith, few are greater and have caused more believers to abandon their faith than the problem of evil. Even more have probably never had any faith because of it. How can a loving, powerful God allow so much evil and suffering in the world?

Believers and nonbelievers alike wrestle with this question, although in very different ways. Thoughtful nonbelievers struggle with the compelling reality of evil. Events like the Holocaust and institutions like slavery seem much more than the mere unfolding patterns of a purposeless nature. Nonbelievers often bristle against the conclusion that morality is an illusory and ungrounded evolutionary artifact, in which case there may be no basis to complain about the unfairness of suffering. Believers, in contrast, battle with the apparent contradiction between God's goodness and the suffering in the world. A world created and superintended by a loving God should not experience horrible events like the Holocaust.

The problem of evil has no simple answer; alas, it also has no complex answer. In fact it has no satisfactory answer whatsoever. If it did, the smart philosophers and theologians of yesteryear would have resolved it already. Nevertheless, many thinkers have developed helpful insights that give us ways to look at the problem. And the evolutionary picture of the world, surprisingly, actually provides some of this help. We will see in this chapter that this perspective on origins actually makes the problem of widespread evil in nature less threatening to faith than the alternatives.

As we grapple with the question of evil, we must first recognize that humans cause much—but not all—of it. Humans, not God, murder, torture, defame, persecute, embezzle and rape. Because humans exercise a genuine free will, they do terrible and immoral things. But free will is essential if the world is to have meaning. Robots have no free will, of course, and in some science fiction scenarios they can do many things just like us. Sometimes science fiction stories feature robots that resemble humans so closely we can't tell the difference. But few people would allow that the activities of robots are meaningful. They may drive cars, talk to children, even rescue women in trouble and kill bad guys like in *Terminator II: Judgment Day.* But, as they operate from a *program* and not a *free will,* we conclude that their activities ultimately have no meaning to them. They can be neither brave nor cowardly, moral nor immoral, happy nor sad because they are just following their programming. They are lawnmowers with on-board computers—three-dimensional cartoon characters carrying out the will of their creators. For creatures to engage in genuinely meaningful activities they must have the freedom to choose or not choose those activities.

Understood in this way, Christians see free will as a gift from God—a gift that brings meaning to life. Free will is also essential if humans are to relate meaningfully to God. For humans to truly love God, other humans, themselves or their pets, they must be free to choose or reject that love.

Because we are *free,* we can choose between real options. Because we are *sinful,* we can choose evil that in principle God could conceivably block. But for God to stop all the evil in the world caused by humans, our freedom would have to be removed and with it our capacity to truly and genuinely love. God, by these lights, cannot give us free will while at the same time restraining us from evil acts. They are a package deal.[2]

What About Evil in Nature?

Believers wrestle with another kind of evil, *natural* evil. Volcanoes erupt and bury villages. Tsunamis inundate coastal cities and drown their inhabitants. Children fall off cliffs. Poisonous snakes bite babies. Lethal viruses and bacteria kill vast numbers of innocent people every year. Plagues have ravaged human societies for millennia, ending the lives of millions of people in calamities of such magnitude that they were often interpreted as divine judgments.

The problem of natural evil relates in an interesting way to the theory of evolution. The natural world, we now understand only too well, has some terrible creatures in it, and it is hard to imagine God intentionally designing such nasty things. Many of us have watched mosquitoes land on our arm and wondered why such annoying creatures need to exist. Often those that land on our arm actually do cease to exist! If we think about it at all, however, it is hard to picture God thinking up this creature and then deciding to create it.

In 1860 Darwin raised this general concern in a letter to the American biologist Asa Gray:

> I cannot persuade myself that a beneficent & omnipotent God would have designedly created the Ichneumonidae [wasp] with the express intention of their feeding within the living bodies of caterpillars, or that a cat should play with mice.[3]

The wasps that bothered Darwin were quite remarkable. They lay their eggs inside the body of caterpillars, and when the eggs hatch, the baby wasps nourish themselves by eating the internal organs of the caterpillar. But—and this seems especially disturbing—they come into the world programmed with an instinct to consume the internal organs of their hosts in the order that ensures their hosts live as long as possible. This seems like the stuff of horror movies, not Mother Nature. Closer to home and often even inside our homes, cats raise similar problems. Why do cats torture their prey before they kill it? Do we have to imagine that God provided cats with an instinct to provide the most violent death imaginable for mice, rather than disposing of them efficiently en route to eating them?

Some Christians try to wriggle off this particular hook by arguing that the unpleasant aspects of the world are the consequences of human sin: byproducts of the Fall. This is an appealing argument in which all the good things in nature—the song of the birds and the beauty of the flower—can be attributed to God, and all the bad things in nature—the poison of the snake and the sting of the bee—can be attributed to human sin. This intriguing point of view, unfortunately, cannot be reconciled with what we know about the history of life.

Advocates of young earth creationism argue that their position resolves the problem of natural evil, but to accomplish this they have to make some implausible proposals. One such proposal is that no animals were carnivorous before the Fall. For starters, as we noted in earlier chapters, this position is not the most reasonable reading of Genesis, nor can it be squared with science. But even if these challenges could be met, the proposed solution requires considerable imagination and far-fetched speculations that go well beyond the biblical account of the Fall. We have to suppose that almost every animal on the planet had its way of life dramatically transformed by the curse. Sharp teeth and poison glands—and the genetic code to produce them—had to pop into existence, since animals were now going to start killing each other for the first time. Thorns had to suddenly appear on bushes. Vast numbers of vegetarian animals became carnivorous. And all this had to happen without leaving any trace in the fossil record. Teeth fossilize very well, and if there were a time when all animals were vegetarian, there should be some evidence for this in the fossil record.

Furthermore, for the pre-Fall world to be completely free from every kind of physical death, it could not have been an orderly free world at all. Somehow, according to this interpretation, no animal could ever fall from a cliff until Adam and Eve sinned; no tree branch could break off and fall on a rabbit or empty out a nest of baby birds; no chipmunk could fall into a stream and drown; no hoof could ever land on a grasshopper. Imagining a world like this is, quite simply, impossible.

We need not consider these options, however, as they have been ruled out by careful measurements of the age of the earth, which show it to be billions of years old and occupied by countless life forms long before human beings appeared. One obvious example is the dinosaurs, which went extinct some sixty-five million years before humans arrived on the scene.

It is abundantly clear that death and suffering had been present for literally billions of years before the appearance of humans. So how could human sin be responsible for this? This claim collapses and can only be rescued by desperate moves, like the claim that later events can cause earlier ones. Surprisingly, there are those so eager to make human sin the explanation for all the evils of natural history that they make this paradoxical claim. William Dembski, for example, makes this argument in *The End of Christianity.*[4]

If human sin is not the culprit responsible for all the evil in the world, what is? Why do animals eat each other? Did God intend to create a world where extinction would be the fate of almost all species? Did God dream up, design and then create truly dreadful creatures?

The wasps that bothered Darwin have an impressive set of sinister instincts. The existence of so much well-designed evil in nature has to be taken seriously in any attempt to understand God's relationship to the world. And certainly, envisioning how a good God would create such things drives home the problem of evil with renewed force.

This perspective on the problem of evil creates special challenges for intelligent design. ID theorists highlight the remarkable features of nature and fashion them into arguments for the existence of a designer. The existence of so many intelligently designed *sinister* creatures in nature suggests that the designer displayed great creativity in fashioning intricate cellular machines cleverly designed to harm humans and even kill them. The AIDS virus is incredibly well designed and has successfully fought off a billion dollar pharmaceutical industry trying to eradicate it. The bacteria that wiped out a third of the population of fourteenth-century Europe during the black plague was certainly well designed.

Readers familiar with ID literature will recall that the various "irreducibly complex" structures in nature that get all the attention are either helpful to humans, like the blood-clotting mechanism, or delightfully cute, like the little motor on the bacteria called the flagellum, which spins to provide locomotion. These are effective examples to use, of course, which is why they work so well to inspire belief in a designer. What we need, however, is a broader consideration of complexity in nature which includes complex machines that are not warm and fuzzy, and appear designed to inflict pain or induce death.

We must not, of course, ascribe the origin of these sinister features of the natural world to God. The God of the Bible would not play a cruel joke on mice by designing cats to torture them. (What did the mice ever do to deserve that?) Nor would this God give the bacterium that causes bubonic plague its remarkably well-designed power to kill some two hundred million people—many of them innocent children—over the past two millennia.

So we return to the question we have been hinting at: Where did these sinister designs originate? Some respond too quickly that they come from Satan, but this is too glib a response from a Christian perspective. To ascribe the creation of *anything* in nature to Satan is to elevate Satan from a *creature* to a co-creator of the world with God. This claim is quite heretical from a technical point of view. No distortion of Christian theology can accommodate the idea that Satan created portions of the world. To suggest this is to embrace a famous heresy known as Manichaeism that St. Augustine flirted with as a young man.

Geneticist Darrel Falk summarizes the problem: "The Satan that we know from Christian theology is not a designer of life's machinery. Those who wish to believe this are free to do so, but they have moved onto an island of scientific fantasy and perhaps even theological heterodoxy."[5]

So if we can't blame human sin, Satan or God for these sinister designs, what are we going to do? Here, evolution actually makes a valuable contribution to Christian theology. In contrast to the challenges that evolution has posed to traditional belief—and we do not mean to minimize those—we now find that evolution has a most useful positive and constructive insight to offer.

How Does Evolution Help Faith?

Science has shown with remarkable clarity that nature has builtin creative powers. Imagine, for example, the state of the universe after the big bang when there was nothing but particles rushing through space at great speeds. The relentless tugging of gravity gradually gathered these particles into an interesting hierarchy of structures—stars, galaxies, clusters, super-clusters and so on. We can say that gravity possessed the creative power to build a star from a collection of atoms. As Christians we affirm, of course, that such powers—which include the power to create things both remarkable and boring, simple and complex, wonderful and terrible—come from God, but they are wielded by nature, as the example of gravity shows. This does not imply that nature is personal or has intentions. Gravity does not look at a cloud of atoms and think, *I should make a star out of this stuff.* But it reflects the reality that nature does things—often quite remarkable—without assistance from outside.

Consider, for example, the tides that sculpt rock formations. Water goes back and forth, twice daily for thousands of years, and produces spectacular works of natural art. In much the same way, mutations and natural selection sculpt the characteristics of species over the millennia. Species like beavers dramatically alter the landscape as they fell trees to build their dams. This view of nature is a traditional theological concept that understands that God works through *secondary* as well as *primary* causes.

This picture gets even more interesting when we note that many processes in nature exhibit a genuine unpredictability that looks, for all the world, like *freedom.* The behavior of electrons, both inside and outside atoms, is genuinely free in the sense that the behavior is *not* the result of outside influences or prior history. An electron in an outer atomic orbit, for example, can jump into any of several inner orbits, and there is nothing that determines which option it will choose. We know from atomic physics that an electron in a hydrogen atom will eventually move to the first orbit. That is the stable and "normal" location. This electron can be stimulated to jump out to a much larger orbit, but it will always return, just as the proverbial arrow shot into the air comes back to earth.

Suppose, for example, that the electron is in atomic orbit number nine, just as poor demoted Pluto is in planetary orbit number nine. One of the ways that atoms differ from solar systems is that their electrons will jump into smaller orbits the first chance they get. And they will not stop jumping until they are in the smallest possible orbit with an open spot for them. An electron in orbit number nine might jump all the way to the smallest orbit. Or it might jump to orbit three first and then one. Or orbit seven followed by six and then to one. There are many possibilities.

The great shock of quantum mechanics was the discovery that identical electrons in identical atoms will "choose" to do different things. Or the same electron will do different things at different times. The electrons appear to be acting freely, like children jumping down the stairs. The brave older boy leaps all the way to the bottom in one leap, but his little sister jumps on each step. The other children jump in different intervals that appear to be freely chosen and not predictable. They all end up at the bottom, but they freely choose their own path to get there.

The freedom possessed by electrons is completely different from the freedom of a tossed coin. The so-called freedom of a tossed coin is no freedom at all—it is simply our ignorance of the relevant factors that determine the outcome. If we had such knowledge we would know the outcome of a coin toss with the same certainty that we know a child's helium balloon will sail into the sky if he or she lets go of the string.

The freedom of electrons is real. Many of the smartest scientists of the twentieth century, including Albert Einstein, were profoundly skeptical that nature could really be like this. They raised every imaginable objection. Einstein phrased his objection as "God does not play dice," refusing to believe that the world was genuinely free and unpredictable. But all these objections were swept away in the stunning success of the new theory that proved, eventually to almost everyone's satisfaction, that nature possessed a genuine freedom.

These and other related considerations force us to look at nature in new ways. We can no longer suppose, as eighteenth-century physicists were inclined to do, that the future is already determined. The actual future is *open* and cannot be known simply as a predictable extension of present processes. On the other hand, nature's freedom is constrained in ways that assure that the world will be stable. Planet earth will not suddenly plummet into the sun, and Mount Everest will not detach and float off into space.

That nature has freedom is highly provocative and theologically suggestive. God created the world with an inbuilt capacity to explore novelty and try new things, but within a framework of overall regularity. This is the way the world is.

The key point here is that the gift of creativity that God bestowed on the creation is theologically analogous to the gift of freedom God bestowed on us. Both humans and all creation have freedom. Our freedom comes with a moral responsibility to use it properly. But that does not prevent us from doing terrible things. The freedom God gave humans was exercised in the construction of gas chambers at Auschwitz and Dachau, and in the destruction of the World Trade Center on 9/11. But because humans have freedom, we do not say that God created those gas chambers. God is, so to speak, off the hook for that evil.

In exactly the same way, outside of the moral dimension, when nature's freedom leads to the evolution of a pernicious killing machine like the black plague, God is off the hook. Unless God micromanages nature so as to destroy its autonomy, such things are going to occur. Likewise, unless God coercively micromanages human decision making, we will often abuse our freedom.

Falk and fellow geneticist Francisco Ayala have both argued "a God who creates by direct intervention must be held accountable for all the bad designs in the world." They argue that evolution mitigates this problem by suggesting that "God set up a world in which evolution (by natural selection) brings about bad designs."[6] This is a subtle point and easy to miss.

Intelligent design leader William Dembski, for example, challenges this distinction. On the one hand there is the freedom of God to create and be accountable for the result. On the other there is the freedom of God to grant nature some of its own freedom, apart from God's freedom, just as we have free will in most theological traditions. In this case God is not accountable for the results. Dembski denies that these are really different: "In the one case, God acts directly; in the other, indirectly," says Dembski. "But a creator God, as the source of all being, is as responsible in the one case as in the other."[7]

Dembski creates the following analogy to dispute this distinction between things God is accountable for and those he is not:

> We never accept such shifting of responsibility in any other important matter, so why here? What difference does it make if a mugger brutalizes someone with his own hands (i.e., uses direct means) or employs a vicious dog on a leash (i.e., uses indirect means) to do the same? The mugger is equally responsible in both cases. The same holds for a creator God who creates directly by intervening or indirectly by evolution.[8]

This analogy misses the central theological point of the argument: *freedom.* When God, as a loving Creator, *withdraws* from complete sovereign control over his creatures and grants them freedom, this means—in ways often difficult to understand—that those creatures can now act independently of God. They are free to not be robotic automatons, puppets or trained attack dogs. In the case of the Holocaust—the classic example of human evil—we *always* do exactly what Dembski says we *never* do: we shift the responsibility for that evil from God to the Nazis. Such reflections have long characterized Christian thinking about the problem of evil. All we need to do now is enlarge this general concept to include the sorts of things that nature is doing on its own.

Not all Christians are comfortable with the idea that nature has freedom, of course. For those more deeply rooted in the Reformed theological tradition—and this includes Dembski—any solutions to the problem of evil that compromise God's sovereignty only create other theological problems. Theological traditions that do not place the same emphasis on God's sovereignty find these explorations less threatening.

Have We Solved the Problem of Evil?

We hasten to point out that the speculations offered here do not *resolve* the problem of evil. We still have to ask why God would not intervene and prevent great evils like the Holocaust or the black plague, but in even posing this question, we have acknowledged that God could only do this by intervening and interrupting the unfolding course of events—events that do not find their origins in God. If we can accept that God's plan includes granting genuine freedom to people, to be exercised for good or evil, then we can accept that the Holocaust, no matter how terrible, can occur within the larger framework of God's purposes for his creation.

This argument is not new; it is a traditional argument recast to help us see that evolution can be a friend to faith. We can disagree, of course, about how helpful it is in mitigating the problem of evil. As we stated earlier, there is no resolution to the problem of evil. We would certainly argue, however, that evolution makes the problem of evil less serious. Those instincts that drive cats to torture mice can emerge naturally and freely from the evolutionary process. They need not originate in the mind of God.

The skeptical theist Martin Gardner makes a similar argument in an essay titled "Evil: Why We Don't Know Why." Gardner considers evil to be an insoluble problem for belief in God, but one we must simply accept as a part of the mystery of our existence.[9] The Cambridge University theologian Frederick Robert Tennant puts it like this: "Evil is the price we pay for existing. Moral evil," he adds, "is the necessary accompaniment of free will. Physical evil is the necessary accompaniment of structured world."[10]

In the seventeenth century the great philosopher and mathematician Gottfried Leibniz made a variation of this argument when he acknowledged that there are many terrible things in the world but that this was still the "best of all possible worlds." Perhaps, argued Leibniz, this is actually the very best way to create a world that is interesting and meaningful like this one. Bland worlds without the possibility of disasters or worlds where God constantly intervened to prevent disasters were, in Leibniz's view, inferior to this world.[11]

None of these arguments makes it easy to fully accept and understand why a loving God would allow suffering from natural disasters or diseases, or from parasites that evolved via natural selection. John Polkinghorne refers to these unfortunate byproducts of evolution as a consequence of physical evil.[12] They cause destruction and pain, but are not linked to human agency.

The very mechanisms that God used to create humans—like the "misspelling" of a gene during cell replication—also produce pain and suffering when those misspellings lead to cancer. Likewise, the same forces that produced a life-sustaining planet, including the laws of physics, chemistry, weather and tectonics, can also produce natural disasters. As with the free will of humans, God cannot constantly intervene in these areas without disrupting the inherent freedom of the creation and disrupting his consistent sustaining of all the matter and energy in the universe. Without this consistency, science would be impossible, moral choices would be subverted and the world would not be as rich with meaning and opportunity.

If God blocked the consequences of human moral choices (e.g., committing murder) and natural events (e.g., tsunamis) every time they led to evil results, moral responsibility would disappear and the natural world would become incoherent. Imagine a world where we could feel totally free to lose our temper and, in a fit of road rage, run down jaywalking teenagers, confident that God would whisk them away at the last minute so we couldn't actually harm them.

Does the Reality of Good and Evil Create an Argument for the Existence of God?

Evil, as we have seen, challenges the existence of a good and loving Creator. But it also challenges those who deny the existence of God in such a way that the *unfairness* of evil can be interpreted as support for God's existence.

Those who complain about injustice and the unequal distribution of happiness and suffering appeal to a larger transcendent structure that provides an order of some sort for the way that things are *supposed* to be. Most of us agree that there is something wrong when children in poor nations starve while rich nations squander money and resources. But what is the basis for such claims? In a purely materialistic world, where life is viewed by some as nothing more than complex assemblages of molecules, what obligation does one molecular assemblage have for another? We don't scold the tree for using all the sunlight and withering the bush struggling in the shade beneath it. Why should we scold the fat-cat banker for having an abundance of resources when homeless children have none?

To be fair, many atheists and agnostics have created ethical systems that encourage generosity and promote fairness.[13] And many are themselves persons of great integrity, demonstrating in their own lives that they are able to find an adequate grounding for their personal morality. Furthermore, many Christians are self-indulgent and enjoy great wealth they have no intention of sharing. But in those ivory towers where thoughtful people try to make sense of the world, it often seems that a moral order with God in it is more robust than one without.[14] Nevertheless, while we affirm these sentiments, we caution against making too much of this argument.

Invoking God to explain features of reality like the apparent existence of moral standards is an ambiguous exercise at best. Many critics charge, with some justification, that this is just the old god-of-the-gaps strategy, where we plug God as an explanation into whatever holes are not filled with adequate scientific explanation. Darwin filled one of the biggest such holes with the theory of evolution. But there is no consensus that Darwin's theory can adequately explain our sense of morality.

There is ample evidence that natural selection supports cooperation and basic altruism, but there are strong forms of altruism—think Mother Teresa or Oskar Schindler—that appear to go beyond what evolution can explain. This creates a gap in our scientific picture of the world that can be filled by invoking God. But this is risky, as the historical example of William Paley makes clear.

Prior to Darwin, there was a widely held belief, enthusiastically endorsed by Darwin as a young scientist, that the complex physical features of nature required God for their explanation. This viewpoint was articulated in Rev. William Paley's popular work *Natural Theology, Or Evidences of the Existence and Attributes of the Deity Collected from the Appearances of Nature,* published in 1802. In a famous passage, which Darwin had memorized, Paley wrote:

> In crossing a heath, suppose I pitched my foot against a stone, and were asked how the stone came to be there: I might possibly answer ... it had lain there for ever.... But suppose I had found a watch upon the ground, and it should be inquired how the watch happened to be in that place; I should hardly think of the answer which I had before given, that for any thing I knew, the watch might have always been there.[15]

Paley's oft-quoted passage goes on to make the logical inference that there must be a watchmaker to explain the watch, because of its clear evidences of intelligent design.

Darwin's controversial achievement was to provide a natural mechanism by which such remarkable features of nature could arise. Some considered his theory to be an affront to faith, but only because arguments like those of Paley had become accepted as appropriate foundations for belief in God. Any time an apologetic argument is framed and presented as an *alternative* to faith as a foundation for belief, there is a danger that further advances in knowledge will undermine this argument. Such advances will *appear* corrosive to faith, but only because a theologically suspect argument for the existence of God has been framed and promoted as legitimate.

To the degree that the faith of nineteenth-century Victorians rested on arguments like those of Paley, that faith was destined to be challenged by Darwin's theory. Richard Dawkins makes this point with his usual effrontery in *The Blind Watchmaker: Why the Evidence of Evolution Reveals a World Without Design:*

> An atheist before Darwin could have said, following Hume: "I have no explanation for complex biological design. All I know is that God isn't a good explanation, so we must wait and hope that somebody comes up with a better one." I can't help feeling that such a position, though logically sound, would have left one feeling pretty unsatisfied, and that although atheism might have been logically tenable before Darwin, Darwin made it possible to be an intellectually fulfilled atheist.[16]

Dawkins assumes here that Paley's arguments for the existence of God were the primary barriers to disbelief, and once those barriers came down, atheism was home free. Belief in God is much more complex than this, of course, and we must not let amateur theologians like Dawkins do our theology for us. But his point is well taken.

Now what about the problem of morality? Is the existence of moral standards similar to the existence of a watch, pointing to a Creator who created it in the form that we find it? Or is it like the existence of our big brains, which can now be explained through evolution? The perspective we present here is helpful because we affirm that God could certainly work through natural processes to produce moral standards. However, there simply is no compelling theory at the moment to support this, although Robert Wright has produced an intriguing hypothesis in *The Evolution of God.* Wright makes a compelling case that human beings have a well-developed ethical sense that developed naturally because the world is organized in such a way as to reward an increasing generosity of compassion and concern for others. He suggests that the hypothesis that God created the world to evolve like this is a reasonable explanation.[17]

Theologically, the notion that God might work patiently over vast periods of time to bring about a particular result is quite reasonable, but, of course, science cannot contribute much to this.

What we would suggest, based on present understandings, is that the prevalence and universality of moral standards is entirely *consistent* with the existence of God and may even be a pointer to that God. Christians have every right to affirm that their worldview is *coherent* and not at odds with experience. But we shouldn't be too eager to build a logical argument for God's existence on this foundation, lest that foundation be dismantled at some later point. On the other hand, without God undergirding the moral order, there is little reason to think of it as a moral order at all. Morality cannot be grounded in atoms and molecules.

If we accept that our moral instincts are somehow *real*—that our visceral responses to genocide or the rape of a child are more than mere emotional reactions—we are confronted with a reality that transcends the natural order.[18] Science can tell us only how the world *is.* We can note, for example, that most humans have a strong reaction to the rape of a child. But the compelling sense that such an act is *wrong* cannot be grounded in our evolutionary history. If we accept the reality of such moral laws, then we must ask about their origins. God is a reasonable conclusion to such an exploration.

Isn't God's Existence Part of God's Nature?

In many faiths God's origin is presumed to be straightforward and not in need of justification. Christianity teaches that God is eternal and thus had no beginning. The Psalms speak clearly about God's eternal nature, affirming but never defending God's existence:

> Before the mountains were born
> or you brought forth the earth and the world,
> from everlasting to everlasting, you are God.
> (Psalm 90:2)

These verses, and others like them, highlight the complexity of God's relation to time, at least from a biblical perspective. Theologians have debated the relationship of God to time for centuries and come to no consensus. No doubt they will continue to debate without consensus, for it seems most likely that the question of God's relation to time is probably not a question we can answer. Physicists, in particular, have thought a lot about time and are not sure exactly what it is.[19]

In one view God is the creator of time itself, and thus exists *outside* of time, seeing all of history at once. Bible verses like Psalm 90:2 support this view. On the other hand, this view has been critiqued by biblical scholars, including Clarke Pinnock, John Sanders and Gregory Boyd, who note that God is portrayed in Scripture as acting *in* time, rather than watching everything from outside the unfolding course of events.[20] For example, when God is negotiating the fate of Sodom and Gomorrah with Abraham (Genesis 18:16-33) or lamenting having created humans at the time of Noah (Genesis 6:5-8), God certainly seems fully embedded in time and responding to the events as they are occurring. But of course, since we know so little about either time or God's nature, there is no compelling reason to reject the claim that God could not be *both* outside of time and capable of acting within it. In this case it is entirely possible for God to be the creator and originator of all that is, while still involved in the processes of creation.

Arguments based on religious doctrine, of course, are rarely adequate for nonbelievers. In fact, many Christians also reject arguments based on God's timelessness since even timeless beings may need explanations for their existence. Many believers affirm belief in God as a matter of *faith,* while rejecting arguments attempting to prove that belief on other grounds. One can certainly believe in God without any obligation to affirm any particular argument for God's existence.

In any event, if God is the creator of all things and yet also requires a cause, we face an infinite regress of causes—the problem of the logical dominoes. The only way to avoid this infinite regress problem is to state—as Christian theology has always done—that God is the *first cause* and is entirely self-existent, meaning the reason for God's existence is contained within the very definition of God.

While this viewpoint may be attractive, it is not convincing to skeptics who charge that this entire argument is just verbal sleight of hand. God is simply defined in whatever way is needed to create an argument that God exists. Such skeptics often counter with the idea that the universe contains within itself the reason for its own existence. If that could be true of God, why couldn't it be true of the universe?

There is reason to be skeptical about the commonsense intuition that everything must have a cause or that everything must have a reason to be as it is. This perennial assumption has been challenged by the physics of the twentieth century that uncovered a mysterious quantum world. In this reality things often do not appear to have any reason to be the way they are.

The commonsense assumption that everything must have a cause or a reason to be as it is also suffers from what is called the *fallacy of composition.* We commit this fallacy when we assume that properties of the parts apply to the whole. For example, just because every member of the human race has a mother, we cannot infer that the human race itself has a mother. Similarly, a collection of spherical things would not itself have to be spherical; the collection of all finite numbers is not itself finite; and so on. In discussions about the origins of the universe, we would not say that because every individual part of the universe has a cause, the universe as whole must have a cause. On the other hand, just because an argument commits a fallacy does not mean that its conclusion is false.

Of course, modern cosmology provides powerful hints that our universe did have a beginning, regardless of the logic surrounding such intuitions. This realization has opened up exciting new conversations about origins. In some ways, a universe with a beginning seems to beg for a cause. But if the universe came into being from nothing, it becomes deeply problematic to speak of anything having caused the universe to exist, at least if the cause is also limited in time and space.

Some cosmologists argue that our universe is the result of an uncaused quantum fluctuation. Such fluctuations do not have causes in the traditional sense, so they argue this does away with our universe needing a cause. But there is a significant problem with this argument: the vacuum that fluctuates is not nothing. Quantum vacuums—which are what we get when we remove from space all the particles and energy—are *real.* They have activity, laws and rules. Our universe may have fluctuated into existence from such a vacuum, but the vacuum remains unexplained. The argument, like the reality it misunderstands, turns out to be entirely vacuous.

Cosmologist Lee Smolin suggests in *Life of the Cosmos* that black holes can give birth to new universes. He proposes that our present universe emerged out of a black hole in some other "metauniverse." And perhaps our universe is presently birthing new universes. Such a process, while clearly speculative, provides a caution against extrapolating from commonsense notions of causality to philosophical conclusions about the nature of all of reality.[21]

If Not Proof, How About Plausibility?

The difference between the theist and atheist positions on this topic is subtle: by assuming that everything—including the universe—has to have a cause, the atheist is left with a dilemma of what or who that first cause might have been. For the theist, the answer is God, but a satisfactory reason must be found for why God should be exempt for the need for a cause. Such a response is available through the traditional Christian affirmation that God is not limited in space and time, and therefore the argument of needing a first cause loses its power.

On the other hand, if not everything needs to have a cause, the theist and atheist have no grounds for arguing this part of their case.

We suggest, however, that the argument can be reframed in a way that is more sensitive to postmodern intuitions about causation and the importance of starting points. Suppose, as a religious believer, you ask the question, What kind of a universe is *most compatible* with my belief in an eternal God? In this case the response *affirms,* but does not *prove,* the reality of God. The universe we experience *appears* to have had a beginning; it *appears* to be finely tuned for life; it *appears* to have a place for love and purpose. These appearances affirm as *plausible* your prior belief in God.

Now suppose you start from the atheist assumption: the universe must not really be as it appears.

It cannot have a real beginning, be tuned for life and love, and purpose can't be anything other than illusory epiphenomena—the curious byproducts of chemistry and physics. The whole picture has a claustrophobic bleakness that, while perhaps real, is so unappealing that it demands a higher level of evidentiary support.

Bertrand Russell, one of the most brilliant and ruthlessly honest atheists of the twentieth century, captured this sense of despair in *A Free Man's Worship:*

> That man is the product of causes which had no prevision of the end they were achieving; that his origin, his growth, his hopes and fears, his loves and his beliefs, are but the outcome of accidental collocations of atoms; that no fire, no heroism, no intensity of thought and feeling, can preserve an individual life beyond the grave; that all the labors of the ages, all the devotion, all the inspiration, all the noonday brightness of human genius, are destined to extinction in the vast death of the solar system, and that the whole temple of man's achievement must inevitably be buried beneath the debris of a universe in ruins—all these things, if not quite beyond dispute, are yet so nearly certain that no philosophy which rejects them can hope to stand. Only within the scaffolding of these truths, only on the firm foundation of unyielding despair, can the soul's salvation henceforth be safely built.[22]

In contrast to this view, theists affirm that the wonders encountered in the world are real, that they belong and are a reflection of the glory of the Creator whose mysterious power upholds everything.

So Where Are We?

The world disclosed by modern science is far subtler and more nuanced than the world in which philosophers and theologians have lived for the past few centuries while formulating their arguments about the mysterious relationship between God, humans, the physical world, time and causality. Nevertheless, no development in contemporary science poses a particular challenge to the view that God is Creator. And some developments, like the discovery of fine-tuning in the physical laws, are supportive of traditional affirmations.

The commonsense assumptions that have historically undergirded this entire discussion, however, need reconsideration in the face of recent scientific developments. We must be intellectually humble in making claims about God as Creator. But we should also state confidently that denials that God is Creator are fraught with even more irresolvable difficulties and ultimately provide a less satisfactory grounding for a worldview in which meaning and purpose play important roles.

The arguments in this chapter are made within the cultural context of postmodernity, which is skeptical of hard-and-fast proofs based on unbridled faith in human reason. We suggest instead that religious believers, long nervous about the corrosive effects of science on their beliefs, take heart. The theory of biological evolution mitigates objections to religious belief based on the problem of evil, and the conclusions of cosmology make theism a more natural foundation for a worldview than atheism.

6

Why Is Darwin's Theory So Controversial?

So God created the great creatures of the sea and every living and moving thing with which the water teems, according to their kinds, and every winged bird according to its kind. And God saw that it was good.

GENESIS 1:21

Many people mistakenly believe that before Darwin published *The Origin of Species* in 1859, all Christians generally affirmed a literalist interpretation of Genesis and that this view dated back to the birth of the church in the first century. While the majority of Christians did accept the idea of a young earth around the turn of the nineteenth century, many significant examples reveal this was not a unanimous consensus, and, more importantly, few thought this position was particularly important. In fact, the idea of an old earth had become increasingly popular among educated Christians throughout the half-century leading up to *The Origin of Species.*

We emphasize the important difference between a *belief widely shared by Christians* and a *belief cen-*

tral to Christian theology. Many Christians once believed the earth was young and continue to do so. But this is certainly not an argument that such a belief is important to theology. By analogy, most Christians think three wise men visited Jesus at his birth, but this idea, like belief in a young earth, is not scriptural and not an *important* belief.[1]

How Did Christians Respond Initially to Darwin's Theory?

A second misconception is that Christians greeted Darwin's theory with immediate hostility because it was incompatible with belief in a young earth. While Darwin's explanation of origins did inspire significant discussion, little of the theological controversy related to the age of the earth. In fact, educated Christians had been comfortable with an ancient earth for decades. The concerns about evolution revolved around two more abstract issues.

The first issue was the concern that Genesis seemed to describe a creation in *decline* instead of *progress.* For centuries Christians had viewed the world around them as deteriorating steadily from a Golden Age at the beginning of time, and now Darwin was claiming that life had been steadily advancing from simple to complex, and humans—the pinnacle of creation—were recent arrivals.

The second issue related to the broad question of reconciling Darwin's *mechanism* of evolution with the character of God revealed in Scripture. For example, because Darwin's theory provides an explanation for the diversity of life today, it appears that God played less of a role in the act of creation. This is still a popular topic for discussion, as we have seen. But in the immediate wake of Darwin's publication of his theory, there was little concern that young earth creationism was the only proper interpretation of Genesis.

What About the Beliefs Before Darwin?

Darwin did not invent the idea of evolution. By the time *The Origin of Species* was published, the idea of evolution in many forms was already popular, and the essentially synonymous term *development* was used to refer to changes in society or the history of the solar system.[2] What's more, it was widely accepted—even among conservative Christians—that the earth was much older than previously thought.

Most of the groundwork for this understanding resulted from the Progressionist movement earlier that century. This movement responded to the rapidly growing roster of fossil discoveries generated in part by the spades and shovels of the industrial revolution digging roads and tunnels all over Europe. In particular the Christian worldview had already dealt with the shock of extinction, as they discovered fossils of animals, like dinosaurs, that were no longer in existence.

Extinction was unusually troubling because it seemed incompatible with God's purposes, especially as revealed in the story of Noah's flood. If God valued animals enough to have Noah mount a heroic rescue effort to prevent them perishing in the flood, then surely God would not look the other way as they gradually died out after the flood. Furthermore, an idea called the "Great Chain of Being" had become popular as a way to illustrate the wisdom of how God had created life forms in a grand pattern that stretched from simple dead matter through plants, animals, humans, angels and on to himself. The poet Alexander Pope summarized this idea elegantly in his epic poem *Essay on Man:*

> See, thro' this air, this ocean, and this earth,
> All matter quick, and bursting into birth.
> Above, how high progressive life may go!
> Around, how wide! how deep extend below!
> Vast chain of being! which from God began,
> Natures aethereal, human, angel, man,
> Beast, bird, fish, insect, what no eye can see,
> No glass can reach; from infinite to thee,
> From thee to nothing. On superior pow'rs
> Were we to press, inferior might on ours;
> Or in the full creation leave a void,
> Where, one step broken, the great scale's
> destroy'd:

From Nature's chain whatever link you strike,
Tenth, or ten thousandth, breaks the chain alike.[3]

Written in 1734, Pope's poem, from which this passage is taken, illustrates the challenge provided by extinction where "one step broken, the great scale's destroy'd." In the decades that followed, Christians were forced to confront the reality of extinction and the associated evidence that the past extended back in time more than a few thousand years and was much different than the present.

As the geologists inspected the evidence from the past, it became clear that there had been a progression through time. Older rocks had no human fossils in them and were dominated by simpler animals than what we see today. The rocks were telling some kind of story of how life had progressed from earlier, more primitive forms to the present.

This Progressionist perspective encouraged the major shift from the view of a young earth to an old one. And all this occurred decades before Darwin and had nothing to do with evolution. Most Christians at the time were quite content to align their understanding of Scripture with these ongoing discoveries. Two views, in particular, became quite popular as straightforward ways to reconcile a literal reading of Genesis with the new discoveries.[4]

As described in more detail in chapter two, the first of those views is known as the *day-age* theory (see p.70), which interprets each of the days in the Genesis creation account as a long span of time, perhaps a geological epoch. A second interpretation is known as the *gap* theory (see p.71). which claims that although God was creatively active in increments of twenty-four-hour days, the Scriptures skip over a vast period of time between God's initial creation of heaven and earth, and the later Edenic creation described in Genesis.

Both of these views allow a literal interpretation of Genesis that was still compatible with the scientifically determined age of the earth, which was turning out to be way more than the six thousand years that had been estimated by everyone from Isaac Newton to Bishop James Ussher, who stated that the creation occurred in 4004B.C.

What Was the Response to Darwin?

The day-age and gap theories prepared the way for Darwin by laying groundwork for new readings of Genesis.

Darwin's theory did, however, raise deeper questions than how to interpret Genesis. These controversial questions spanned both theology and science: Was there any room left for God's creative activity? Could natural selection explain how traits were inherited in the evolutionary process? Could it determine the cause of variation in the first place? Could it explain everything in nature without invoking the supernatural? If it could, what was God's role?

Darwin's ideas took decades to be fully accepted by the scientific community, and as long as there was scientific skepticism, many Christians did not feel threatened by a theory that might actually wither on its own scientific vine. However, the reaction of those Christians that did weigh in, sometimes just hypothetically, in case Darwin turned out to be right, was more accepting than many suppose.[5]

To understand the difference between the immediate response to Darwin and the vigorous opposition that arose much later, we have to understand two very important characteristics of the half century that followed the publication of *The Origin of Species:*

1. The scientific community was broadly skeptical that blind, unaided natural selection could do all the work that Darwin assigned to it. Most scientists accepted that Darwin and others had established that evolution had indeed occurred, but they were inclined to see the evolutionary process as *purposeful* in various ways. In one view, called *orthogenesis,* evolution was the unfolding of prescribed patterns and thus was easily seen as nothing more than the mechanics of God's creative plan. The aspect of evolution with the greatest potential to offend most Christians was not the claim that species could evolve but that the process might be undirected, purposeless and, by implication, without meaning. But this was not how many of Darwin's generation, in-

cluding leading scientists, understood his theory.[6]

2. American Christianity's dramatic struggle with nineteenth-century biblical scholarship opened a divide between liberal or modernist expressions of the faith and more conservative, traditional expressions. The modernists emphasized the social gospel while downplaying—and even denying—the virgin birth, resurrection and divinity of Jesus. Because the modernists were enthralled with science, they tended to be evolutionists, which naturally made conservatives uncomfortable with evolution.[7]

The United Kingdom provides some examples of Darwin-friendly Christians, including a member of the Royal Society, William Henry Dallinger, who was a Wesleyan pastor from 1861 to 1880 and later was president of Wesley College. In a presentation to the British Methodist Conference in 1887, Dallinger admitted an "unreserved acceptance of evolution."

Regarding the random variations and adaptations of the evolutionary process, Dallinger explained, in distinctly non-Darwinian language comforting to Christians:

> Every instance of what such writers as Darwin are obliged to write of as "contrivance," or "adaptation" throughout the universe [are] but factors of related harmony in a stupendously vast interlocked "mosaic" of design, which in its

entirety has a "final purpose" too great for man to see.[8]

Another British advocate of theistic evolution was Sir George Stokes, the Lucasian Professor of Mathematics at Cambridge University from 1849 to 1903—a position held by both Isaac Newton and Stephen Hawking. Although Stokes hesitated to apply evolution to the human species, he made considerable effort to clarify that "even an extreme adoption of evolution is not inconsistent with theism," and there was no need to assume that each species arose by individual creative acts.[9]

The National Academy of Sciences in the United States was initially reluctant to accept Darwin's theory. However, the theory was widely accepted by the 1880s, thanks mainly to the Christian biologist Asa Gray. Gray's religious beliefs compelled him to argue in favor of certain modifications to Darwin's theory, but he worked energetically to ensure that evolution was well received in the United States.[10]

American theologians and biblical scholars, of course, pondered the compatibility of Darwin's theory and Christian doctrine. As in Britain, American scholars of religion were already comfortable with views like day-age or gap theories, in large part because the ambiguous structure of the Genesis creation accounts seemed to invite flexible readings. However, their initial responses to Darwin were varied. Some viewed evolution simply as God's method of creation, anticipating later views like that being presented in this book. Others argued that since Darwin's theory explained away the apparent design in nature, it was compatible only with atheism and therefore should be rejected by Christians.[11]

With time, however, even some of the more conservative biblical literalists became comfortable with Darwin's theory, finding plausible ways to reconcile the Bible and evolution. The great Princeton theologian B.B. Warfield (1851-1921) is an especially helpful case study because his strong views on the complete inerrancy of Scripture are often cited by today's most conservative young earth creationists and other fundamentalists.[12] And yet Warfield writes, "I am free to say, for myself, that I do not think that there is any general statement in the Bible or any part of the account of creation, either as given in Gen. I & II or elsewhere alluded to, that need be opposed to evolution."[13]

By the end of the nineteenth century, as Darwin's theory became more broadly accepted by scientists, many theologians accepted evolution except for the human species, which they argued possessed properties, like morality, that evolution could not explain. Some of their hesitancy derived from concerns that evolution could undermine morality and even the larger social order, or that evolution could conflict with Christian claims that human beings were created in the image of God.[14] Although Warfield shared some of these concerns, he also acknowledged the following:

> The upshot of the whole matter is that there is no necessary antagonism of Christianity to evolution, *provided that* we do not hold to too extreme a form of evolution. To adopt any form that does not permit God freely to work apart from law and which does not allow miraculous intervention (in the giving of the soul, in creating Eve, etc.) will entail a great reconstruction of Christian doctrine, and a very great lowering of the detailed authority of the Bible.[15]

Despite his acknowledgement of difficult issues with evolution—including the creation of Eve—his stance on the interpretation of Scripture was clear. Although committed to the plenary verbal inspiration of the Bible, he did not see any need for a wholesale rejection of Darwin's theory of evolution.[16]

Interestingly, at the end of the nineteenth century almost nobody was arguing directly in favor of a young earth with an age of less than ten thousand years. Enthusiasm for this view was largely confined to the Seventh-day Adventists, who followed the writings of their founder Ellen G. White, considered a prophet by the Adventists. In one passage, White described a vision she had of the creation of the earth. In another vision God revealed to her that Noah's flood produced the fossil record.[17] Early Adventists could thus reconcile the geological data found in the early nineteenth century with a literal reading of the flood story of Genesis 6–8, by assuming that Noah's flood did all the work. White's vision was destined to grow dramatically in its influence, however, as it was embraced first by rank and file fundamentalists and then by most evangelicals.

How Did Young Earth Creationism Become So Popular?

As we saw in chapter two, the early twentieth century movement known as "fundamentalism" did not embrace young earth creationism and was even friendly toward versions of evolution. *The Fundamentals* included a commentary on evolution written by George Frederick Wright, a proponent of the day-age theory who occasionally collaborated with Asa Gray. Wright put no emphasis on Noah's flood as an explanation of the geological data. That idea was circulating only among the Seventh-day Adventists.

The widespread creationism of today gained traction as an anti-evolution movement that simply reinvented the "flood geology" of Ellen White's vision. This flood geology was presented in a series of ambitious books by a self-taught but quite convincing amateur geologist named George MacCready Price. By the early 1960s, Price's ideas, updated by Whitcomb and Morris in *The Genesis Flood,* were becoming the mainstream belief of antievolutionists of many theological stripes. This shift can be attributed mainly to timing.

The one-hundredth anniversary of Darwin's publication in 1959 brought with it a cry from academics to make the public more aware of Darwin's theory, which was still largely excluded from public school textbooks. Around the same time, the Soviet Union launched the Sputnik satellite, a spectacularly successful threat to the United States' leadership in science. As a result the government funded the Biological Sciences Curriculum Study (BSCS), a project that produced a series of textbooks presenting evolution without reservation as the central organizing principle of biology.[18] Many conservative Christians at the time saw this as an attempt to "ram evolution down the throats of children."[19]

Whitcomb and Morris saved the day by providing Christians with an alternative to evolution that was, as they described it in *The Genesis Flood,* faithful to both science and the Bible.[20] They explained how Noah's flood accounted for the geological evidence for an older earth, making sweeping claims about the nature of fossilization that later generations of creationists could not confirm. Soon after, small groups of conservative Christian scientists began to form in support of this research, trying to create a scientifically viable model of earth history consistent with their reading of the Bible. They came to be known as young earth creationists and referred to their flood geology as scientific creationism.

To gain acceptance for their ideas in public schools the creationists dropped references to the Bible and argued that they had a viable model that could stand alongside the conventional picture of earth history provided by the mainstream scientific community. Their model explained the standard evidences for evolution, including the order of the fossils, the apparent age of the earth and the similarities between organisms. The movement grew, and by the 1970s the term *creationism* had been reduced and redefined to encompass a set of ideas that included elements from Ellen White's visions.[21] This is essentially the viewpoint promoted today by groups like Answers in Genesis and The Institute for Creation Research.

Young earth creationism has successfully developed some popular arguments that almost everyone interested in this topic is familiar with. Darwin's theory has been fighting off challengers since it first appeared in 1859, but the challengers have now acquired the upper hand in many parts of the United States.

In the remainder of this chapter we will look at three different scientific challenges that evolution has faced. The first problem relates to the age of the earth, which we examined in detail in chapter two. This was dealt with and effectively dismantled by the very people that had proposed it in the first place. The next problem deals with the second law of thermodynamics, which has been inappropriately but effectively used to challenge evolution for decades. The final challenge relates to the origin of life, a genuine scientific problem that is nowhere near being resolved.

All of the challenges to evolution fall into one of these three categories:

1. Scientific problems that have been fully resolved but continue to circulate because their supporters are not current with the scientific literature or do not respect that literature.
2. Scientific problems that are not really problems but are based on enduring misunderstandings that seem resistant to clarification.
3. Scientific problems that are recognized by the scientific community, which expects to resolve them using the tools of science.

Is There Scientific Evidence Against Evolution?

In the century and a half since Darwin published *The Origin of Species,* critics have energetically developed scientific reasons to reject evolution. One of the first such "scientific" refutations came from physicists contemporary with Darwin who were sure that the earth was about 100 million years old—not old enough for evolution to have produced the variety of species known to exist.

The physicists' argument—led by Lord Kelvin, the greatest physicist of his era—was based on the theory that the earth had originated in a molten state and had been cooling ever since, radiating heat energy out into space. The heat remaining in the ground, evidenced in hot geysers, volcanoes and other geothermal phenomena, was left over from this early molten period. Simple analysis of cooling rates revealed that the earth could not possibly be billions of years old because it then would be much cooler now.

The argument of the physicists apparently refuted Darwin's theory by proving that the earth was too young to have produced the known array of life forms, both present and past.

Within a few years, however, physicists discovered radioactivity. Many atoms were found to spontaneously disintegrate into other atoms, releasing heat in the process. Vast quantities of radioactive material in the earth have been releasing heat since the earth originated, partially balancing the heat being radiated into space as the earth has cooled from its original molten state. New estimates for the age of the earth that took this new heat source into consideration produced a value compatible with Darwin's theory. Radioactive dating would go on to become a remarkable clock, providing its own independent measures of the age of the earth. It would also serve the evolutionary biologists well in helping them determine the ages of many fossils.

This episode in the history of science is remarkable. The very unquantitative science of biology, with its messy and inarticulate narrative of natural history, had triumphed over the mathematical theories and equations of the physicists.

In the century since this initial victory, Darwin's theory has met many subsequent challengers and overcome all of them. These challenges, however, continue to circulate among many nonscientific laypeople convinced that there is a reliable body of scientific evidence that refutes evolution.

Does Thermodynamics Disprove Evolution?

One of the most popular arguments against evolution is that the theory contradicts the second law of thermodynamics, one of the best-established laws in all of physics. The second law states that the disorder of a system or, more technically, its *entropy* increases over time. This law has plenty of familiar everyday examples, which can lead to the mistaken impression it is simple and easy to interpret. Buildings break down over time, cars rust out and food spoils. In all such cases, the disorder increases with time, but the opposite is never true. Buildings don't strengthen themselves, rust piles never rise up to become cars and no amount of waiting will make rotten food edible again. We seem to be surrounded by examples of the second law.

Evolution, in contrast, seems to be exactly the opposite of this. A simple one-celled life form becomes multicellular and then grows in complexity, getting steadily bigger and more elaborate, adding limbs, lungs, kidneys, a heart with a valve system, and eventually a big brain. This process, as described, seems as unlikely as a pile of rust rising up to become a car—a steady billion-year-long violation of the second law of thermodynamics.

This objection, however, is grounded in a simple misunderstanding of the second law. Fortunately it is easy to understand the problem, which is not always the case with physics.

The second law of thermodynamics states that *any isolated system will increase its total entropy over time.* The key phrase here is *isolated system.* Understanding exactly what this means is the first step to the key insight that evolution is in no way at odds with this and, in fact, has little to do with the second law.

What Exactly Is Entropy?

Entropy is a measure of the *disorder* of a system. The disorder of a system is a statement of how independent all the parts of the system are or, more technically, how many different states the system can possibly be in. A marching band with everyone in lock step is an example of a system where the parts are not all independent. Such a system does not require a lot of information to describe, for example, the location of the musicians: "Everyone shall be marching three feet behind the person in front of them and two feet from the people on either side." Such a description would be adequate to locate the members of the band, assuming we don't care who is in each location. That same group of people in a mall shopping independently would require a lot more information to specify their locations: "Musician at diet soda section in aisle four at Walmart; another one in front of line at Starbucks; another in changing room two at Lord & Taylor." Once the original pattern has broken down, the marching band becomes disordered, which means that it takes a lot more information to describe their locations. Their entropy has increased.

As noted earlier, the entropy of a system tends to steadily increase over time. An example analogous to the marching band—and one to which you could actually apply the relevant equations—would be the collection of molecules in a bottle of perfume. Take the cap off a bottle of perfume and then do nothing. Gradually the smell of the perfume will fill the room as the molecules spread around. Describing the distribution of the molecules after they are out of the bottle is like describing the marching band after it has gone shopping.

As perfume molecules spread throughout a room the entropy of the room increases because the perfume loses its organized distribution in the bottle. Related to this is the impossibility of the perfume molecules ever spontaneously reassembling in the bottle. While not technically impossible, the probability that the molecules would all meander randomly back into the bottle at once is so small that we never expect to see it.

In this example the room with the open perfume bottle is treated as an *isolated system,* which means there are no external sources of energy present to provide possible routes to less disordered systems.

No system, however, is *completely* isolated from outside influence. The question is always whether it is *sufficiently* isolated for the second law of thermodynamics to be helpful in understanding what is going on. We can see the significance of this by looking at the same examples. Consider the marching band. After the performance they appear to all go their own way to more or less random locations. Imagine you were tracking them all as blips on a GPS device as they headed off to the mall—you would see the blips moving about almost like perfume molecules coming out the top of the bottle along apparently random and independent trajectories. But suppose the marching band members had agreed to reassemble six hours later for another performance. What would this look like on your GPS? You would see the blips converge to the same spot and line up in an orderly pattern—almost like time was running in reverse and the disorder was decreasing. What is going on?

The answer, of course, is simple: there is a *plan* in place, and the members of the marching band are not mindless perfume molecules; they are fully capable of using the various energy sources at their disposal—buses, taxis, bicycles—to carry out the plan. They can drive or walk back to the original location, but the energy that makes this possible comes from *outside*—from the food they ate in the mall, for example.

Almost every imaginable system in nature has outside input. Even gravity can provide a source of energy that influences the order of a system that might otherwise appear closed. To see this, suppose that, instead of perfume molecules, we were releasing helium atoms into the room. The helium atoms, being lighter than the air, would all rise to the ceiling. If gravity could be shut off, the helium atoms would disperse randomly, but the moment gravity reappeared, they would all migrate to the ceiling, as the heavier atoms fell downward. Gravity thus functions as an outside source of energy, producing order by layering the atoms and molecules in the room based on how heavy they are.

In the same way, sunlight can produce order. The most important example is photosynthesis, where the energy from the sunlight is used to make sugars from carbon dioxide and water. If we were just watching the process with no knowledge that invisible energy from the sun was pouring in, it would appear mysterious—simple molecules steadily assembling themselves into complex molecules, like rust rising up to become a car. There is no mystery, however, and the second law of thermodynamics is not violated because the system is not isolated. In fact, if we include the sun in our "system" here, we discover that the disorder (entropy) of the sun is increasing furiously as it releases copious quantities of energy in all directions, a tiny bit of which falls on the earth and drives the photosynthesis process.

The only truly isolated system is the universe as a whole and, from a narrow technical perspective, the second law applies *perfectly* only to the universe as a whole. The total disorder of the universe—the amount of information needed to describe its state—is always increasing. But there are many smaller systems on the earth that are close enough to being isolated that the second law is an excellent approximation to what is going on.

How Does the Second Law Apply to Evolution?

Readers who have understood the previous examples should now be wondering how in the world the second law of thermodynamics can possibly relate to evolution. And they are right to wonder this. Biological systems are so far from being isolated that it is virtually impossible to even apply the second law.

With biological evolution the system being considered is not the universe as a whole but the earth, and really just the surface layers of the earth where life flourishes. The earth, of course, is not an isolated system, which means, at the most basic level, an increase in order can occur on earth as long as there is an energy input like light from the sun. Energy input from the sun can give rise to an increase in order on earth, including the formation of complex molecules, as we saw with photosynthesis, and even organisms. As evolution unfolds on earth the sun becomes increasingly disordered and the total order of the solar system and the universe is still decreasing.

The claim that evolution violates the second law of thermodynamics is thus grounded in an understandable but nonetheless profound *misunderstanding* of where the law applies. This arises quite naturally when we forget that the law is based on an *equation,* not on a *sentence.* The equation for entropy is S=kLn (Omega). S is the entropy, k is a constant, and omega is equal to the number of different states of the system. "Ln" is a mathematical operation, typically done with a calculator, and means to "take the natural log of omega." When the perfume molecules are all in the bottle, the number of possible states is small, since their location is so restricted. (Think of *states* as "places to be.") As they migrate out of the bottle the number of states grows steadily. S, or the entropy, will grow in accordance with the growth in the number of states, like the formula says.

Confusion arises when we explain the mathematical equation in words. We say "Entropy is a measure of disorder that must always increase." Immediately we nod our heads picturing our houses that get messy, our cars that rust away or our clothes that get dirty. But these are not helpful examples or even good analogies since they are all so far from being closed systems. Similarly, when we picture a bacterium and a person, and suppose that the second law prevents the former from evolving into the latter, we are misunderstanding the law. It is hard to even figure out what omega would be for a person, much less determine what it would mean to say "omega was always increasing."

Applying the second law to living creatures is thus all but impossible. There is no clear meaning to the entropy of a frog, other than the trivial observation that isolating it from outside sources of energy will not be good for its health! The kinds of systems that can be usefully analyzed with the second law are much simpler.

Living organisms, such as frogs, are not so much unified wholes as they are collections of subsystems. In the development of life on earth, for example, a major leap occurred when cells mutated in such a way that they clumped together making multicellular life possible. A simple mutation allowing one cell to stick to other cells enabled a larger and more complex life form. Probably energy from jostling water carried the cells together so they could stick to each other. Such a transformation does not violate the second law of thermodynamics any more than superglue violates the law when it sticks your fingers to the kitchen counter or to each other.

As was the case with the systems involving perfume and marching bands, consideration of simple examples in evolution—like the emergence of multicellularity—can be helpful. Suppose that a herd of buffalo, for example, found themselves experiencing a prolonged drought. One buffalo experiences a mutation that improves their ability to retain water and use it more efficiently. This advantage improves their health and enhances their reproduction. As a result they have more offspring and eventually this mutation spreads to the entire population, making them better adapted to their increasingly dry habitat. How does this improvement to the buffalo *violate* the second law? How does it even *relate* to the second law?

The claim that evolution violates the second law of thermodynamics is thus seen to rest on a faulty interpretation of the law, a misunderstanding that is easy to dismiss once we consider the sorts of things that happen in natural history that make up the evolution of life on earth.

But What About the Origin of Life? Isn't the Origin of Life Highly Improbable?

Closely related to the concern that evolution violates the second law of thermodynamics is the claim that natural causes are incapable of producing life. This claim is more significant in that it is not based on any misunderstanding. Even simple life forms have an arrangement of molecules that seems unlikely to arise by chance. We note in passing, though, that the origin of life is technically outside the purview of Darwin's theory of evolution. The theory of evolution deals with the *development* of life, not the *origin* of life from nonlife. Nevertheless, it is a critically important part of the origins story and thus deserves careful consideration. And it is, to be fair, often included in discussions of evolution.

We take up the question of the origin of life to illustrate what is involved when a legitimate scientific challenge is posed. We cannot dismiss this as a simple misunderstanding, nor can we offer some deep insights into how to resolve it. But we can show our readers how scientists who believe in God think about a problem like this.

Scientists are confident, for various reasons, that the earth began in a molten state about 4.5 billion years ago.[22] Initially the earth would have been too hot for the chemical reactions necessary for life to occur. Those conditions would not have existed until roughly four billion years ago. Some time after that life first appears.

From all we know about the state of the earth three to four billion years ago and what we know about the complexity of the building blocks of life—DNA, RNA, amino acids, sugars—no adequate hypothesis for the spontaneous origin of life has yet been found. Because the topic has fewer potentially useful applications than other areas of science, less research has traditionally been performed in this area. The research is also very complicated, since we don't know exactly what earth was like before the significant changes introduced by life began to take place, nor do we have any idea what form the first self-replicating systems took.

Scientists approach this challenge from several perspectives, all of which offer tantalizing insights but no compelling resolution.[23] The absence of an answer today, however, does not mean there will be no answer tomorrow. Scientists agree that this is a complex problem that has simply not been solved. Like the problem of dark matter and the origin of Pluto, it represents an intriguing mystery. It is a mystery, though, that most scientists, including many that believe in God, think the methods of science will ultimately be able to solve.

The fact that an explanation for the origin of life is currently elusive does not mean divine intervention is the only possible explanation or even the best explanation. Nor is there any more reason to invoke divine action in this case than for the origin of Pluto. There are many unexplained mysteries in the natural world; the origin of life is simply a compelling example. Unless we believe that divine intervention is the preferred explanation for everything that science can't explain, we should look to contemporary science to see what insights might exist into this complicated problem.

We hasten to add, however, that our perspective on such questions is that we are looking for the mechanisms by which God worked through the laws of nature to bring about his intentions.

What Does Science Know About the Origin of Life?

The first step in opening up this problem is to clarify what is meant by life. We must resist the temptation to picture the first life forms as little creatures running about. The first forms of life on earth were probably very different from what we would call life today, and would have been little more than assemblages of molecules engaging in chemical reactions with other molecules. We also must not think of life as necessarily containing the DNA double helix.

The *main* property required for early life is self-replication, which does not have to be based on DNA. The earliest self-replicating systems could have been made out of DNA, RNA or some other building blocks. Since RNA can both carry information and act as an enzyme, the "RNA World" hypothesis has gained favor in origins science. But RNA is notoriously unstable, making it difficult to understand how this could be the full answer. It is likely that important new discoveries will have to illuminate this process before it will seem convincing.

The key feature of such systems would be their ability to gather chemicals from the local environment and make copies of themselves. The compounds used in this process would be organized around carbon, used by all life on earth as an essential building block.[24] Carbon is the simplest element capable of forming the complex molecules prevalent in life forms. Scientists agree that carbon was almost certainly involved in life from the beginning.

The importance of carbon to life is reflected in the very language of biochemistry that categorizes compounds containing carbon as *organic.* Exploring the natural mechanisms that create complex organic compounds is a main focus in research on the origins of life.

As mentioned earlier, some four billion years ago earth had cooled to the point where it became hospitable to life. Within about 150 million years, evidence indicates that the first single-cell life forms appeared.[25] Where did these organisms come from? And what were their capabilities?

Although we don't know the path that led to these early forms of life, their simplicity leads scientists to believe they were bacterial, perhaps similar to bacteria of today. It also appears that DNA had emerged as the "information molecule" by this time. So the earth would have had simple bacterial life, reproducing itself with DNA.

But Where Did These Organisms Come From in the First Place?

Charles Darwin proposed an original "warm little pond" hypothesis for the origin of life:

> It is often said that all the conditions for the first production of a living organism are present, which could ever have been present. But if (and Oh! what a big if!) we could conceive in some warm little pond, with all sorts of ammonia and phosphoric salts, light, heat, electricity, etc., present, that a protein compound was chemically formed ready to undergo still more complex changes, at the present day such matter would be instantly devoured or absorbed, which would not have been the case before living creatures were formed.[26]

Although little more than speculation with no science to back it up, Darwin's hypothesis—if we can even call it that—has been widely criticized as if it were proposed as some sort of final answer.[27] Soviet biochemist Aleksandr Ivanovich Oparin, however, revisited this idea and proposed that life originated in an environment that lacked oxygen but was energized by sunlight.[28] Without living plants to create oxygen it is most likely that the early earth had very little oxygen. Such speculations are the basis of the research of life's origins, including the famous and much-maligned Miller-Urey experiment.

In 1953 Stanley Miller and Harold Urey tackled the problem of the origin of life by reproducing the conditions believed present on earth when life originated. They zapped a mixture of water and inorganic compounds like methane and carbon dioxide with electricity to simulate a primitive ocean experiencing light-ning. They produced complex organic compounds including amino acids, the building blocks of protein.[29] This result catalyzed further experiments and some hopeful researchers became optimistic that the solution to the mystery of life was about to unfold.

A 1961 discovery by Joan Oro demonstrated that an essential component of DNA—adenine—as well as several amino acids could be formed by heating hydrogen cyanide in water-ammonia.[30] Though this work contributed useful pieces to the puzzle,[31] these sort of Miller-Urey experiments have fallen far short of explaining how life originated.

How Did Life Arise?

Explanations remain speculative for how amino acids, nucleotides and sugars were formed, how they assembled in the form of DNA and RNA, and then how these building blocks of life came to replicate themselves and acquire the enzymes to facilitate this process. In fact, there is no consensus about what kinds of experiments will be most helpful in illuminating the origins of life. Most likely life arose just once, perhaps as a scientifically improbable event from our perspective, but this event might have occurred in a variety of places and along a variety of pathways.

Many interesting ideas are being researched, however, including the deep sea vent theory,[32] radioactive beach theory[33] and crystal or clay theory.[34] Another opinion, held by Francis Crick and others, is that the best explanation for life on earth is that it came from another planet.[35] However, this type of explanation only pushes the question further back: How did this life originate on this other planet? A compelling explanation of the origin of life here on earth has not yet emerged.

Conclusion

The study of life's origins is an exciting area of research. The jury is still out—way out—on how life first emerged. A simple response would be to give an old-fashioned god-of-the-gaps explanation: some supernatural force, namely God, must have intervened to bring life into being. We do not categorically exclude this, but would encourage our readers not to jump to this all-too-easy solution.

Consider the timeline of these scientific quandaries. Life on earth appeared approximately 3.85 billion years ago, yet serious scientific study of its origins began just sixty years ago. A convincing scientific explanation may still emerge in the next fifty years. Though the origin of life could certainly have resulted from God's direct intervention, it is dangerously presumptuous to conclude that the origin of life is beyond discovery in the scientific realm simply because we do not *currently* have a convincing scientific explanation.

Although the origin of life is certainly a genuine scientific mystery—as opposed to a pseudo-scientific problem, like how evolution overcomes the second law of thermodynamics—we suggest that this is not the place for thoughtful people to wager their faith. This kind of logic would mean God worked in some special way at this stage only to allow the evolutionary process to move through later developments that did not require divine intervention. In contrast, the perspective we are advancing maintains that God's original and elegant plan for the universe may well have included the potential for life to arise without necessarily requiring later "supernatural" engineering to jumpstart the process. In this view, God's sustaining creative presence undergirds all of life's history from the beginning to the present.

7

What Is the Fine-Tuning of the Universe, and How Does It Serve as a Pointer to God?

The heavens declare the glory of God; the skies proclaim the work of his hands.

PSALM 19:1

As we approach the end of this book, we turn to two of the most engaging and provocative questions in all of science—the apparent fine-tuning of the universe for life, and the growing evidence that the evolution of life on our planet had an unfolding pattern. We do so deliberately because these topics provide an encouraging new paradigm for Christian thinking about science.

We will look at the fine-tuning of the laws of physics in this chapter, exploring the evidence that the universe is curiously biofriendly. In chapter eight we will look at biological evolution and whether it displays similar patterns of purposeful directionality. Taken together, cosmic fine-tuning and evolutionary directionality bring a coherence to the history of the universe and create a grand narrative that takes us from, in the words of one pundit, "the big bang to the big brain."[1]

For religious believers the discussion surrounding big bang cosmology and biological evolution can seem endlessly and discouragingly *defensive.* It sometimes seems we are constantly protecting traditional doctrines, finding plausible reinterpretations and discovering new compromises that we can make to accept what science has discovered about the world without rejecting faith.

This discouraging perspective may be an overreaction to the collapse of the more traditional views of creation. For most of the history of Christianity origins was viewed as a supernatural event—an act of divine origination. Even those who did not interpret the Genesis creation story literally, like Augustine, still viewed the origin of the world as supernatural and outside the natural course of events. Certainly the loss of that perspective, which had been at the center of the Christian tradition—and Western civilization—for many long centuries, was disappointing. And it is only natural that we react with a certain sense of loss and search, as many are eager to do, for ways to reject the new and challenging ideas from science that threaten the traditional view.

But now that the dust has settled, so to speak, and many are no longer trying to reverse the tide of scientific progress, we are beginning to see an exciting *new* understanding of origins—of humans, of life, of the earth and of the entire universe—rising out of the rubble of the old misunderstanding. Because we understand science as a genuine part of God's revelation, we are confident and encouraged by these developments.

What Is the Fine-Tuning of the Universe?

Cosmologists have discovered something extraordinary about the universe. The laws of physics have precise properties that make them look like they were designed to enable life. Furthermore, our universe began in a peculiar event called the big bang, which seems to have occurred in just the right way so that the universe being born would one day be capable of supporting life. The ideas that constitute these insights are known as the fine-tuning of the universe.

Fine-tuning looks like a *pointer* to a Creator—not a proof, to be sure, but a suggestive state of affairs. Fine-tuning invites the speculation that an intelligence brought this universe into existence some 13.7 billion years ago, intending that it would one day teem with living creatures. To explain the present state of the universe—with its planets, stars and galaxies—scientific theories require that the physical constants of nature, like the strength of gravity and the electromagnetic force, have a precise character. In the same way the beginning state of the universe has to have its properties, like its density and expansion rate, precisely set.

If any of the physical parameters mentioned here, and a host of others, differ even *slightly* from their actual values, the result is a universe incapable of hosting life. The laws have to cooperate in remarkable ways to make the universe habitable, so many cosmologists have concluded that the universe is finely tuned for life. This observation is also referred to as the *anthropic principle,* a term whose definition varied over the years.[2]

This fine-tuning is seen most clearly in the values of the constants of nature—those boring numbers listed in appendixes in physics books. There are many such constants, including the mass and charge of the electron, the speed of light and the magnetic moment of the neutron. The most important constants determine the strengths of the four basic forces in nature.

One of the most well-established insights in physics is that there are just four different forces in nature, with gravity being the most familiar. All natural phenomena, from the exploding of an atomic bomb to the ringing of a bell, can be completely described, at least in principle, using these four forces. There is no evidence of any phenomena in nature that falls outside this description.

These four forces are:

1. *The strong nuclear force.* This force holds the nucleus together. Since the protons in the nucleus have positive charges that repel each other, some other force must overcome this repulsion and keep the protons together. This force, the

strongest of the four, is like superglue, which is irrelevant when objects are not "touching" but becomes powerful when they make contact.

2. *The weak nuclear force.* This force is responsible for radioactive decay. It can turn one of the neutrons in the nucleus into a proton. An electron is created by this event to ensure that no charge is created. (The total charge after the conversion has to be the same as before.)
3. *The electromagnetic force.* This force is responsible for electrical and magnetic phenomena, including holding the electrons in their orbits about the nuclei of atoms.
4. *The gravitational force.* This force holds us on the earth so we don't float away into space, but it is also responsible, over the history of the universe, for gathering matter into stars, stars into galaxies and galaxies into even larger structures.

Each force has characteristics that determine what it does, what parts of physical reality it influences and how strong that influence is. The electromagnetic force, for example, acts on electrical charges or magnetized bodies. The magnet of the earth pulls on the magnet of a compass and lets us know which way is north. The electromagnetic force does not exist between people in the same room, except on rare occasions when static electricity might appear. Similarly, the moon has only a tiny magnetic field, so there is no electromagnetic force of any consequence between the earth and the moon. The force between the earth and the moon is almost entirely gravitational.

The magnitude of the electromagnetic force between two objects depends on three things: (1) the amount of magnetism or electrical charge of the objects, (2) the distance between them—the force is stronger when they are closer, as everyone knows from playing with magnets, and (3) the value of the electromagnetic constant, a number that determines how strong the force is. The first two of these are obvious and natural. We might expect, for example, that a force between two bodies would get weaker as they move away from each other. But the electromagnetic constant is just an arbitrary fact of the universe, and there seems to be no reason why it has the value that it has.

The gravitational force, in contrast to the electromagnetic force, acts on everything in the universe, since everything has mass. The most familiar example is our own weight, a measure of how hard the earth is pulling on us. Our weight depends on how far we are from the center of the earth, our mass and the mass of the earth, and the gravitational constant. Once again there is a constant that determines how strong that force will be. If the constant were greater, then gravity would be stronger and we would weigh more.

At first glance it may appear that these forces are not relevant for biology, and in fact this was the prevailing view until the middle of the twentieth century. But since then this idea has been turned on its head. All biological phenomena depend, in a detailed way, on the nature of these laws. We now understand that if these forces took on even slightly different strengths, the consequences for life would be devastating.[3]

Because the strengths of the physical forces have to be "adjusted" to precise values for life to be possible, we use a musical analogy. Just as the strings on a violin have to be tuned precisely for the violin to produce beautiful music, so the constants of nature have to be tuned precisely for the universe to produce life. This is called the "fine-tuning" of the universe.

What Is the Best Example of Fine-Tuning?

There are many examples of fine-tuning, but perhaps the one that has generated the most discussion is the way that the universe makes carbon, the most important building block in living cells.[4] Two of the four forces we listed earlier, the strong and electromagnetic, collaborate remarkably to enable unusually efficient production of carbon. The forces cooperate to create what looks like a coincidental matchup of energy levels, enabling the production of carbon in stars from the fusing of three helium atoms. This is so intriguing that it repays the effort to understand it.

Most of the heavier elements in the universe were created in stars though *fusion,* which is also the process that provides the energy for the stars to shine. Stars are composed mainly of hydrogen, but because the gravity of a star is so great, the hydrogen atoms are compressed so tightly together that they fuse into helium, the second lightest atom. The helium atoms fuse with other hydrogen atoms to create lithium, the third lightest atom. Two helium atoms can fuse to create beryllium, the fourth lightest atom. And so on down the periodic table, as increasingly complex fusion reactions create heavier elements.

Some steps on the fusion ladder are improbable. For three helium atoms to collide and create carbon, for example, is unlikely, even though carbon is element number six and the masses add up correctly. This is because there is more to the fusion process than just getting the masses to match up.

Every atom has a precise amount of energy, and reactions that don't require the release or absorption of energy go much faster than reactions where the end products have a different energy than the starting products. Under normal circumstances, for a reaction like the production of carbon from helium, the energies would not match up perfectly, and the three helium atoms would come apart before they had time to fuse into carbon. It takes a little extra time to deal with the energy mismatch. But if there is an unusual match of the energies, then the process is much faster.

The strong and electromagnetic forces collaborate to enable fusion. The electromagnetic force opposes the fusion reaction by trying to keep the positively charged nuclei away from each other. (The electrons have all been ripped off by the intense energies and are not participating.) Because of the intense heat in the stars, the nuclei move about rapidly with the possibility that they might overcome this repulsion and smash into each other. If they do then the "glue" of the strong force has a chance to hold them together permanently.

The slightest change to either the strong or electromagnetic forces alters the relevant energy levels, resulting in greatly reduced production of carbon. And carbon, of course, is essential to life, so reducing its production dramatically reduces the probability that the universe will turn out to be habitable. Fortunately, the odd energy matchup ensures that carbon is produced in the quantities needed for a universe that will eventually be friendly to life.

In the 1950s, Cambridge University astronomer Fred Hoyle recognized the precision of this energy match up (called the "carbon resonance") and made the following observation:

> A commonsense interpretation of the facts suggests that a super-intellect has monkeyed with physics, as well as with chemistry and bi-

> ology, and that there are no blind forces worth speaking about in nature. The numbers one calculates from the facts seem to me so overwhelming as to put this conclusion almost beyond question.[5]

Hoyle did not argue in favor of divine creation as an answer. He was an agnostic and hostile to the idea that physicists might invoke God to explain anything. The scientific explanation of carbon's development was readily accessible though, and it was easy for Hoyle to see exactly how amazing the process was. But the understanding of the process provided no insight into why the fundamental forces cooperated so fruitfully to produce the unusual energy matchup. Hoyle's remark illustrates just how puzzling it is that the universe has the exact properties that enable the existence of life.

How Is Gravity Fine-Tuned?

Consider also the strength of gravity. Shortly after the big bang occurred, the matter in the universe was randomly distributed. There were no stars, planets or galaxies—just atoms swirling about in the dark void of space. As the universe expanded, gravity pulled ever so gently on the atoms, gathering them into clumps that eventually became stars and galaxies. But gravity had to have just the right strength—if it was a bit stronger, it would have pulled all the atoms together into one big ball. The big bang—and our future prospects—would have ended quickly in a big crunch. And if gravity were a bit weaker, the rapidly expanding universe would have distributed the atoms so widely they would never have been gathered into stars and galaxies. Without stable stars like our sun, there cannot be solar systems where life can flourish. The strength of gravity has to be *exactly* as it is for stars to form.

But what do we mean by "exactly"? Well, it turns out that if we change gravity by even a tiny fraction of a percent—enough so that you would be, say, one billionth of a gram heavier or lighter when you get on the bathroom scale—the universe becomes so different that there are no stars, galaxies or planets. And no planets implies no life.

The other constants of nature possess this same feature. Change any of them and the universe will move, like Robert Frost's traveler, along a different path. And remarkably, every one of these different paths leads to a universe without life in it. Our universe is friendly to life, but only because the past fifteen billion years have unfolded in a particular way that led to the formation of a habitable planet with liquid water and rich chemistry.

There are many other finely-tuned constants of nature besides the strengths of these forces, and they all tell a similar story. Consider the ratio of masses for protons and electrons, as a final example. The mass of a proton is 1836.1526 times the mass of an electron.[6] Were this ratio changed, the stability of many common chemicals would be compromised. In the end this would prevent the formation of such molecules as DNA, the building blocks of life.[7]

With regard to the development of life on earth, it is sometimes claimed that nature would find a way for life to develop no matter what the circumstances. In this way nature is sometimes said to tune itself. However, the finely tuned properties of carbon are required for nature's ability to "tune" itself, even if it were possible for nature to find some other way to create life. In this way the fine-tuning of later systems depends on the fine-tuning of earlier ones.

Alister McGrath puts it like this:

> [The entire biological] evolutionary process depends upon the unusual chemistry of carbon, which allows it to bond to itself, as well as other elements, creating highly complex molecules that are stable over prevailing terrestrial temperatures, and are capable of conveying genetic information (especially DNA).... Whereas it might be argued that nature creates its own fine-tuning, this can only be done if the primordial constituents of the universe are such that an evolutionary process can be initiated. The unique chemistry of carbon is the ultimate foundation of the capacity of nature to tune itself.[8]

What About the Fine-Tuning of the Initial Conditions?

Fine-tuning is also evident in the initial conditions or the beginning state of the universe. (Actually, we know nothing about the absolute beginning of the universe. When scientists speak of the beginning in this context, they refer to a time period just after the actual appearance of the universe—the earliest time when theories provide insight into what was happening.) The initial conditions of the universe include such information as the expansion energy of the big bang, the overall amount of matter, the ratio of matter to antimatter, the initial rate of the universe's expansion and the degree of its entropy.

Consider the expansion rate of the big bang, to take the simplest characteristic. If it were greater, causing the early universe to expand faster, the matter in the universe would have become too diffuse for gravity to gather it into stars and galaxies. If it were less, so the universe expanded more slowly, gravity would have overwhelmed the expansion and pulled all the matter back into a black hole. The expansion rate was just right—like Goldilocks's porridge—so that the universe could have stars in it. And stars make possible solar systems, in which life can exist.

Another initial condition in the finely tuned universe model was the *density* of the universe.

In order to develop in a life-sustaining manner, the universe must have maintained an extremely precise overall density. The precision of this density must have been so great that a change of one part in 10[15] (i.e., 0.0000000000001 percent) would have resulted in a collapse, or big crunch, occurring far too early for life to have developed, or there would have been an expansion so rapid that no stars, galaxies or life could have formed.[9] This degree of precision would be like a blindfolded person choosing a single lucky penny in a pile large enough to pay off the United States' national debt.

What Do Scientists Say About Fine-Tuning?

Needless to say, these provocative insights carry significant implications for understanding the universe. It appears that out of an unfathomable number of possibilities, our universe is one of few that could support life. Consequently, these observations have led religious believers to conclude that the "heavens display the handiwork of God." We now turn our attention to this extraordinary possibility.

We start by distinguishing these cosmological pointers to God from the arguments for irreducible complexity, which have a superficially similar form. Fine-tuning provides examples of how nature came to possess an inbuilt capacity for the production of complex life. This capacity shows signs of having been built in by a cosmic designer.

In the case of irreducible complexity, however, the argument is that nature does *not* have the inbuilt capacity to produce complex life—that God cannot work *through* the laws of nature, at least as we understand them, to create complex structures but must interrupt the natural course of events to bring about designs that nature cannot bring about.

While irreducible complexity arguments are undermined by scientific explanations when they appear, fine-tuning pointers to God are less vulnerable to dismissal on the basis of future scientific explanations. As a result scientists who engage the question of fine-tuning can't dismiss it with a quick—sometimes too quick!—"we will figure that out shortly" wave of the hand, as they readily do with most irreducible complexity arguments. As a result, there is an interesting set of responses.

For thoroughgoing naturalists, fine-tuning arguments are unsettling, since a straightforward interpretation points toward an intelligent Creator. There are, however, some common naturalist responses that must be considered.

Can the Fine-Tuning Be Explained Without God?

The first response is a nonchalant shrugging of the shoulders with comments along the following lines: "Because humans exist, the laws of nature clearly must be compatible with life. Otherwise, we simply wouldn't be here to notice the fact." A surprising number of scientists seem fine with this argument, but we find it quite inadequate, and indicative of a certain philosophical and theological naiveté on the part of those who respond this way. The philosopher John Leslie exposes the inadequacy of this "no big deal" response in his analogy of the prisoner who survives the firing squad.

Suppose you are to be executed by firing squad. Tied to a post and blindfolded, you hear all the guns go off, but you survive because every one of the marksmen missed. How would you think about this, later back in your cell? As you marvel at your good fortune in having survived all these expert marksmen shooting at you, will you be satisfied to tell yourself: "Of course all of the shots missed; otherwise I wouldn't be here to notice that I'm still alive!"[10] This trivial response could satisfy only someone completely devoid of curiosity. Most people in such a situation would speculate about the possibility of a conspiracy of some sort—a plot behind the scenes orchestrated by someone who wanted to save your life.

In the same way it seems unsatisfactory to say of the universe: "Of course all the laws of nature are finely tuned for life. Otherwise we wouldn't be here to notice." A more logical approach would be to seek out an explanation for why such an unlikely situation exists. A good scientific explanation *satisfies curiosity,* whereas this kind of explanation does nothing to offer any resolution.

A second response is based on a cosmological theory called *inflation,* which predicts that the universe will have a certain precision and balance in the laws, similar to what we notice. The theory of inflation states that in the early stages of cosmological evolution, the universe underwent a period of much more rapid exponential expansion.

By proposing the right kinds of inflation, it is possible to show that some of the previous examples would naturally take on the values we observe. In this way, some of the universe's fine-tuning seems to be explained away.

Whether the universe had a period of inflation is a subject of some debate, but most cosmologists agree that some form of inflation took place and that this could indeed explain some of the fine-tuning.[11] But there is more—or less, actually—to this explanation than meets the eye. What is not always included in the description of these inflation theories is the extra fine-tuning the theories themselves require.

In order to produce the inflation—and the associated values for our universe's physical characteristics—inflationary theories require that some of their adjustable parameters take on precise values. So precise that the problem of fine-tuning remains and is only pushed one step back—the logical domino effect. At present most scientists accept the idea of inflation, but few believe it has resolved the fine-tuning problem.

Another response is that the finely tuned features of our world will someday show themselves to have been inevitable. With an increase in our understanding of physics, it is possible that one day we will discover a so-called theory of everything, through which all other facts of physics will be explained. Such a theory might explain why the universal constants and physical laws have to have such specific values. However, each finely tuned feature of our world puts restrictions on any possible theory of everything that might be developed. In the end, only a few highly constrained theories would suffice, and this essentially creates a fine-tuning problem even for theories of everything.[12]

There is a final, quite extraordinary, response we will consider, known as the multiverse. The multiverse hypothesis suggests that there are many other universes in addition to our own, perhaps an infinity of them, each with different properties and different values for the constants of physics. With enough different universes, we need not be surprised that one of them possesses the specific conditions for life.

Stephen Hawking argues that the multiverse hypothesis is really the only way to get around the implication that our universe has been fine-tuned.

A bottom-up approach to cosmology either requires us to postulate an initial state of the universe that is carefully fine-tuned—as if prescribed by an outside agency—or it requires us to invoke the notion of eternal inflation, a mighty speculative notion to the generation of many different universes, which prevents us from predicting what a typical observer would see.[13]

The proposition of many other universes is fantastic, but many ideas in science, from a moving earth to the big bang, have seemed fantastic when they first appeared. Many quite reasonable scientists, including some Christians, accept the multiverse hypothesis. It is extraordinary, though, and we can only marvel that there are theories that suggest such possibilities. And certainly, such a possibility might explain the puzzle of fine-tuning. But we must keep a few things in mind, before we jump on this explanatory bandwagon.

For starters, the likelihood of ever finding any *evidence* of other universes is remote, since even the theories suggest it is unlikely that information could pass between universes. Scientists concerned that theories need firm empirical grounding can legitimately object to the postulation of entire universes that we can never interact with in any way. Furthermore, there is no guarantee that the process producing all of these universes would randomly set the physical parameters in such a way that every possibility is realized.

It could very well be that there are constraints on the characteristics of these many universes and that the production process itself would have to be fine-tuned to guarantee that we get enough variety in our catalog of universes to ensure that one will resemble our cosmic home. How do we know, for example, that the charge on the electron will be set randomly so that all possible values will be present somewhere in the collection of universes?[14]

How Does Fine-Tuning Relate to Intelligent Design?

We enthusiastically endorse the idea that the universe is intelligently designed, and consider the evidence presented in this chapter to be provocative and compelling. We have reservations about the intelligent design movement. We believe that ID lacks appropriate confidence in the ability of science as currently constituted to find answers to the many questions currently on the table. But this is not the whole story.

We think it is important to acknowledge the real similarities between fine-tuning arguments and arguments made by ID. In our opinion these similarities are such that we might think of ID and BioLogos as two ends of the same spectrum, with broad areas of overlap and agreement in the middle. There is a *tension* between the ends of the spectrum but not necessarily *incompatibility* across the board. Our primary concern about ID is that it promotes the idea that nature has gaps in it that God must intervene to fill. According to ID, nature is powerful and capable of accomplishing much, but some things—like the origin of the bacterial flagellum—require that God must "step in" in an unusual way. This seems piecemeal and incoherent to us. We are more attracted to the idea that God accomplishes these things working through the laws of nature, not apart from them.

On the other hand, we acknowledge that the BioLogos perspective can slip too easily into *deism*—the view that God starts things off and then leaves them to run on their own. Our view is often caricatured—Cornelius Hunter says it makes God a "distant memory"—but this is unfair.[15] As parents, to use a helpful analogy, we have both built playground equipment for our children and then let them play on it without hovering over them constantly. But it is completely wrong to say that we just left our kids to play on their own and became "distant memories." Likewise, God can create autonomous creatures with free will, but that does not imply that God then has to lose interest and wander off to some other project. God can remain engaged with those creatures in any way that God wants.

Even with these acknowledgments, however, we share a broad concern that the Creator God of traditional Christianity cannot be constrained only to acts of origination "in the beginning." And the fine-tuning argument is all about beginnings. The central problem here, which is too involved for the present discussion, is *divine action.* But we claim that this problem is no worse from the BioLogos perspective than any other.

Consider the popular young earth creationism position where God creates everything over six days. Given God's relationship to time, is this really any different than God creating over fourteen billion years? In either case we are confronted with the transcendent mystery of God's action. Is it really any different to ask how God creates a cow in twenty-four hours or twenty-four million years? Or consider the ID problem. If God does intervene in natural history to make a cell, a flagellum, hemoglobin or eyes, how does God do that? How long did it take? Did God do it at the level of the gene or everywhere all at once? Is it any more mysterious to claim that God—technically, an anonymous "intelligent agent"—constructed irreducibly complex structures along the way, than to claim that God constructed such structures by working through the laws of nature?

We submit that *all* Christian positions on origins share a commitment to a mysterious and transcendent divine action, and we might as well acknowledge that we are all in that boat together. The conversation needs to be about what is revealed in the details of the creation, not who can explain exactly how God works (for nobody can). We should all start with the affirmation that the world is the product of a transcendent intelligence and then inspect that world to see what we can find out. Along the way we must content ourselves with partial insights, constantly reminding ourselves that we—BioLogos, intelligent design, old earth creationism and young earth creationism—see "through a glass darkly."

Despite this common ground, we have a major theological problem with ID, however. (We hasten to point out that making comparisons with ID is complicated by the fact that ID is not a unified movement. Under its big tent, for example, we find both young earth creationists and people who believe the earth is billions of years old.) The key central claim of ID that concerns us—and which should give Christians pause—is ID's unwillingness to make specific theological claims. ID does not claim that God is the Creator, as BioLogos does. Rather it claims only that "certain features of the universe and of living things are best explained by an intelligent cause, not an undirected process such as natural selection."[16] Some of the people in the ID camp who affirm this don't even believe in God.

BioLogos, of course—and YEC and OEC, for that matter—also affirms an intelligent being created the world. But BioLogos accepts the conclusions of the biologists that life evolved through natural selection; we believe this is the process God used to create; we affirm this, not because we have theological insights that this is how divine action occurs, but because this is what science has discovered about the creation. Although most advocates of ID agree that evolution, understood as "change over time," has occurred, they deny that the biological process of evolution by natural selection could account for the present complexity of life forms on earth.

From a scientific perspective ID argues that evolution cannot explain *certain* aspects of creation, but it can explain other aspects without reference to the intelligent designer. If, as the ID adherents generally endorse, the intelligent designer is God, this implies that God is relevant to *some* but not *all* aspects of creation, a claim we find peculiar. The parts of creation in need of the designer are those that ID claims are *irreducibly complex.* These parts consist of complex configurations of interacting components organized in such a way that one missing component makes the configurations useless, like a computer without an operating system, or a car without wheels. Such configurations could not have evolved from less complex predecessors, since each simpler version of the system would be useless and dysfunctional. Although ID supporters believe that such findings refute evolution, BioLogos—along with the vast majority of scientists—does not see these examples as a threat to the theory of evolution by natural selection.

Christians should be concerned about embracing ID, because it does not affirm that God is the creator. In fact, they even say that the designing intelligence could be a space alien![17] Of course, virtually all the ID people are Christians who believe the designer is God, but that is not officially a part of ID. BioLogos insists that the design of the world comes from the

God that Christians worship, not a random intelligence.

The second reason Christians should be concerned about ID is that it is trying to work outside mainstream science. The central idea of the entire field of biology is that species have evolved over time via natural selection. To reject this is to reject much of biology. And to try to do biological science without the ideas, theories and tools that the field has developed over the past century is to invite error and confusion. Science is hard enough, even within the system of peer review, grants and professional meetings.

A third concern about ID is that it suggests that design may be detected in some places and not others. In contrast, BioLogos affirms that God is present everywhere in nature and not just in the gaps in our knowledge. God is the ultimate explanation for *everything,* not just the bits of nature that science cannot explain. Indeed, often science fills in a gap in our understanding of nature with a new explanation.

ID seeks to identify objective criteria by which design can be ascertained. The oft-used example of Mount Rushmore being the product of an intelligent agency is a case in point. We can certainly detect that it is designed, and we know that we must invoke intelligent—in this case human—designers to account for it. But our understanding of human behavior has been developed and refined over millennia. We take for granted that the patterns that make up the faces on Mount Rushmore preexist in the minds of the artists who did the work. Our explanation that the faces on Rushmore resulted from intelligent agency is really nothing more than a statement that a pattern has been transferred from the minds of the designers to the side of the mountain. But we suggest that little is truly explained by saying that a pattern has moved from one place to another.

A different example makes this point clearer. Suppose you find your friend with a bullet hole in his head, and you wonder if this was a stray bullet or an assassination. You find a video recording and discover that there clearly was an assassin. So the death was "intelligently designed." But is the assassin on the video the explanation for the death or simply the cause? Scientists would like to *understand* the world, not merely *identify causes.* Unlike the Mount Rushmore example, we lack a ready-made explanation for why an assassin killed your friend. The identification of intelligent cause does not *explain* the phenomena at all. In our view the goals of ID are far too limited.

And when we extend this style of explanation to, say, DNA, it becomes even more shaky. In this case we have no experience at all with "intelligent agents coding information in amino acids." The most we can say is that human agents sometimes do things that bear a faint resemblance to this. And we also have the problem of DNA text that doesn't code for anything and "misspelled" text that used to code for something but got damaged along the way.

Despite these concerns we are quite willing to embrace ID in its central affirmation that the universe is best understood when we allow that there is a mind behind it all. Our preference is that we view this mind as God and incorporate whatever insights might be relevant from theology into our worldview.

We caution, however, that the fine-tuning argument must not be too quickly fashioned into an argument for the existence of God. Like all apologetic arguments it can be undermined by new discoveries and weakened by broad theological considerations. In the latter category we note that the fine-tuning of the universe is just as necessary to produce cockroaches as humans. Here we would add insights from theology that humans are made in the image of God and are a far more reasonable goal of cosmic fine-tuning than are cockroaches. But this goes beyond the science.

Science by itself, however, can say nothing more about the physical universe than that it *appears* like a place where life is not an accident. In his autobiography, *Disturbing the Universe,* Freeman Dyson, one of the greatest physicists of the twentieth century, says, "The more I examine the universe, and the details of its architecture, the more evidence I find that the Universe in some sense must have known we were coming."[18]

Dyson's conclusion provides a welcome counter to the discouraging picture of science constantly undermining the worldview of faith.

The cosmic narrative takes us from the big bang to the origin of life, where it joins up with the story of biological evolution. Biology however is more complex than cosmology, and we are just beginning to see hints of broad patterns in the development of life—the life that is possible only because the universe is finely tuned. We now turn to this fascinating question.

8

Evolution and Human Beings

Then God said, "Let us make man in our image, in our likeness, and let them rule over the fish of the sea and the birds of the air, over the livestock, over all the earth, and over all the creatures that move along the ground."

GENESIS 1:26

The finely tuned universe provides a provocative picture of cosmic evolution, but it would be a mistake to ignore the details of the curious path that this biofriendly universe took from the seeming chaos of the big bang to our remarkable planet. It would also be a mistake to overlook the interesting collateral that was produced along the way. For every star capable of hosting a biofriendly solar system like our own, a billion dead zones appeared along the way; for every earth-like planet revolving happily about its life-giving sun, there are a million sterile orbs where life could never exist; in between the uncountable interesting lights that dot the night sky are vast swaths of emptiness, implacably hostile to any kind of life. And yet, here and there, in our vastly extravagant cosmos, there are earth-like planets orbiting sun-like stars. We live on one such planet.

Our home in this vast cosmos is an exceptional place. The earth is rich in life-sustaining chemicals that are incredibly rare throughout a universe dominated by hydrogen and helium. The average temperature on the earth is comfortably in the range of liquid water when most of the universe is either way too cold—interstellar space—or way too hot—inside or near stars. The sun we orbit has a stable output of energy that threatens neither to freeze nor to incinerate us. To get all this out of the big bang is remarkable beyond belief. And yet here we are. Is the grand narrative of the origin of life a "tale told by an idiot, full of sound and fury but signifying nothing"? Or is this a story of God's purposeful creation?

Did Evolution Have to Result in Human Beings?

If the universe is, in fact, finely tuned for life—all kinds of life, not just human—a question naturally arises: Does life offer any hints of what it may be for? Are there any reasons to suppose that life, as it explores its many labyrinthine pathways, is moving toward anything resembling us? Are we relevant?

The starting point for this question is the recognition that life could have turned out quite differently. The process of evolution is driven in large part by random mutations, so it certainly seems possible that earth could have been home to an entirely different assortment of creatures. In fact, the fossil record tells a long tale of different sorts of creatures—some vaguely similar to us, some very similar to us and many not remotely similar to us. It is far from obvious that we were the distant target of life, once it got started on this planet billions of years ago.

Such considerations can certainly affect our sense of significance, and indeed have been the basis for arguments that we are nothing more than a "glorious accident."[1] These ideas appear on the surface to be inconsistent with the belief in a creator who had human beings in mind.

We can approach the topic of human significance from several directions, both scientific and theological.

For starters, a sovereign and timeless God can certainly create humans through an inevitable process that appears entirely random from within the system, so to speak. While we cannot know how God relates to time, it may be that God's purposes are largely invisible from our vantage point. The common but deeply ambiguous view that God is outside time and sees all of history at once supports the idea that there may be purposes visible from God's viewpoint that are invisible from ours. There may be trajectories of purpose within the universe that we can only dimly perceive or not perceive at all. Perhaps cosmic fine-tuning is such a purpose.

If we take the earth and run its history backward to the big bang and then forward again, ignoring everything unrelated to the earth, the process looks anything but random. Up close, though, the details of the process would look *very* random. Inside the star where the carbon destined for our planet was being forged, the environment would have appeared chaotic beyond belief—so chaotic that an observer would *never* infer that the building blocks of life were being created for later use. Only when we look back from our present position can we see the significance of what was happening in that star. From outside time, this picture would be much clearer because the trajectories of purpose would be fully visible.

Another way to think about God's relationship to evolution is to view God guiding the evolutionary process, working *within* the randomness. In this view, God is *within* time, working through the laws of nature in ways that only become apparent much later when we see how things turned out. Take mutations, for example, the raw material on which natural selection works to produce new species. Mutations appear to be genuinely random occurrences that can be initiated by quantum mechanical events. But quantum mechanical events are unpredictable by their very nature (as opposed to being unpredictable because we don't know all the details, like the rolling of dice). The laws of physics permit quantum events to go in different directions. There is no reason why God could not work within such processes, shaping evolutionary history. What appear to be genuinely random events might actually be the subtle influence of God working within the system of natural law.

Finally, we might also imagine, as a third possibility, that God intentionally integrated freedom in the evolutionary process and chose not to predetermine the detailed trajectory of its many winding pathways.[2] But perhaps there are favored directions within the system that tilt the playing field, so things tend toward certain results. There are many analogies that illustrate this phenomenon.

For example, during the great economic catastrophe that occurred as this book was being written, American car companies almost went bankrupt. The government wanted to strengthen them and introduced a "cash for clunkers" program in which people would get extra cash if they traded their old car for a new one. In between the government's intention and the success of the program was the free will of the car-buying public. Nobody was forced to buy a car, but, as it turned out, many people freely chose to buy new cars, and the car companies' financial health was dramatically increased. Examples like this show that even in a world where free will is a reality, history can have purposeful trajectories.

These are theological speculations that we, as mere scientists, ought not pronounce with any certainty. It does seem to us, though, that there are viable ways to think about God's interaction with the world that open the door to the possibility that God has created through the process of evolution.

The question we would like to address in this final chapter is whether the process of evolution as the account of our origins, understood as God's method of creation, makes us any less significant. Can we be both the product of evolution and "created in the image of God"?

As we begin our considerations, we hope readers will agree with us that the relevant part of our origins is not the story of how we acquired the specific details of our body plan—ten fingers, two ears, one nose—or how we lack a marsupial pouch to carry our newborns or why potty-training takes so long. Nothing about these details is critical to what makes us human. Our humanness is embedded more holistically in our less tangible aspects and could certainly be embodied in creatures that looked nothing like us.

Is Human Evolution an Accident?

The conclusion that we evolved by chance emerges quite understandably—but not necessarily—from the very definition of evolution. Evolution begins with unpredictable mutations of an organism's genetic code that result in organisms that are often slightly different than their peers. As far as science can determine, there are no rules that push or encourage these mutations to take any one direction over another. They seem genuinely random.

The late paleontologist Stephen Jay Gould liked to emphasize this contingent, happenstance aspect of evolution. He argues that we could not be here if an asteroid had not randomly struck the earth and wiped out the dinosaurs: "Consciousness would not have evolved on our planet if a cosmic catastrophe had not claimed the dinosaurs as victims."[3] It seems, therefore, that if the DNA in our history had gone in a slightly different direction, a very different species may have evolved. "Replay the tape a million times from [the] beginning," writes Gould, "and I doubt that anything like Homo sapiens would ever evolve again."[4]

Gould was one of the leading voices in the evolutionary conversation for many years and an influential science writer, so we must take his ideas into consideration. Unfortunately, he held the most extreme position on this question, and because he was such an effective writer, this extreme view became widely known—so widely known that many people believed it was the consensus of the scientific community. Fortunately, there are other views on the question of the inevitability of big-brained creatures capable of consciousness, morality and spirituality.

The opposing view comes from the Cambridge academic that Gould highlights in *Wonderful Life*—the very book where he argues for the happenstance character of evolution.[5] One of the world's leading paleontologists, Simon Conway Morris, presents a completely opposite perspective, arguing that humans, or a human-like species, are actually an *inevitable* part of evolution.

Conway Morris is not proposing a different mechanism for human evolution, merely a different understanding of its possible outcomes. He agrees that slight differences in the history of human DNA would result in different evolutionary pathways. Unlike Gould, however, Conway Morris argues that each possible pathway would inevitably lead to something like the human species.

Conway Morris writes:

> The prevailing view of evolution is that life has no direction—no goals, no predictable outcomes. Hedged in by circumstances and coincidence, the course of life lurches from one point to another. It is pure chance that 3 billion years of evolution on Earth have produced a peculiarly clever ape. We may find distant echoes of our aptitude for tool making and language and our relentless curiosity in other animals, but intelligence like ours is very special. Right?
>
> Wrong! The history of life on Earth appears impossibly complex and unpredictable, but take a closer look and you'll find a deep structure. Physics and chemistry dictate that many things simply are not possible, and these constraints extend to biology. The solution to a particular biological problem can often only be handled in one of a few ways, which is why when you examine the tapestry of evolution you see the same patterns emerging over and over again.[6]

The patterns Conway Morris mentions are referred to as *convergences* in the evolutionary process. In *Life's Solution: Inevitable Humans in a Lonely Universe,* he gives many examples of physical traits or abilities found repeatedly among different species. Normally, such similarities are understood as the result of common ancestry. However, the species in Conway Morris's examples are so distantly related that common ancestry is highly improbable. And in many cases not even these species' common ancestor shared the same trait. The implication is that different species have independently developed similar traits.[7]

Examples of convergence range broadly. One popular and straightforward example is the human eye. Several other species have nearly identical visual systems, including, if you can imagine it, the octopus.[8] Humans and octopuses have separate predecessors, however, neither of which shared this characteristic. The evidence suggests that two different evolutionary paths arrived independently at the same visual system.

If Gould's contingency paradigm is correct, and there were countless possible outcomes, then this example of convergence is all the more improbable. Conway Morris's argument, conversely, is that the laws of nature allow for only a few solutions to any particular problem. It appears the eye has developed independently at least seven times over the course of natural history. Considering the remarkable complexity of the eye, the fact that its appearance seems somehow to be built into the evolutionary process is a provocative insight—one that makes a full frontal assault on the standard picture of evolution as a random and meandering path to nowhere.

If Conway Morris is correct, it suggests that there are favored pathways, and while the evolutionary steps might be largely random, there is a tilt to the playing field that favors one direction over another. At present, evolutionary theorists are unclear on how to incorporate such insights, but they are becoming more accepted as the evidence mounts.

How Does Convergence Relate to Humans?

The important aspect of convergence in this discussion, of course, is the degree to which various human characteristics might be built into the evolutionary process. Conway Morris provides several examples of convergence for traits that are particularly relevant for "human-like" creatures. These examples include our all-important abilities to balance ourselves, detect sounds and, of course, our remarkable skills at processing visual information. There is also evidence that highly advanced features like the human brain are convergent.

Conway Morris, a highly respected expert on evolution and a Christian, argues that Darwin's theory poses no threat to human significance. His provocative but respected research indicates that characteristics like large brains capable of consciousness, language and complex thought would *inevitably* emerge from the evolutionary process: "Contrary to popular belief, the science of evolution does not belittle us.

As I argue, something like ourselves is an evolutionary inevitability, and our existence also reaffirms our one-ness with the rest of Creation."[9]

The exact anatomical features of sentient creatures like us might not be precisely specified by the evolutionary process, of course. The playing field of natural history, as Conway Morris argues, is tilted in the direction of big brains and remarkable eyes, but there is no evidence that evolution prefers hands with five fingers, ears five feet above the ground or noses below the eyes rather than above.

Many find this thought unsettling and strangely at odds with their understanding of creation, which celebrates that God created us "in his image." We suggest that this is due to the influence that actual artistic images have had on our view of God and ourselves. Because God became incarnate in Jesus, who looks like us, we all too quickly slip into the assumption that God also looks like us. After all, sons generally resemble their fathers! Religious art, like the anthropomorphic paintings of God on the Sistine Chapel, feed into this assumption that God looks like us. But we know, upon reflection, that these intuitions cannot be correct. God does not have hands and feet. He is not a bipedal mammal with a big brain and two ears. Whatever meaning we attach to our belief that we are in the image of God, we most certainly cannot claim that our physical bodies somehow resemble God's body.

So How Did God Create Humans?

Scientific evidence can be viewed as compatible with and even supportive of the traditional Christian belief that human beings—or creatures like human beings—are a fully intended part of creation. Since Christians believe that God upholds all of creation from moment to moment, God is the ground or basis for the myriad and subtle nuances of nature responsible for the convergences that give rise to human beings.

God is certainly able to interact with the creation. The unfolding paths of natural history leading to human beings may be the signature of this interaction. God can influence the evolutionary process to ensure his intended result, in whatever ways he wants. Furthermore, an omniscient Creator can certainly create the universe in such a way that natural laws would result in the evolution of human creatures. The actual patterns of natural history may, in fact, be a combination of pathways specified by laws laid down "in the beginning" and the steady infusion of divine creativity.

The scientific evidence supports the idea that the evolutionary process did not *require* steady tinkering and regular intervention from God, although such intervention is not ruled out. This evidence also does not rule out the possibility of God working within the system, although it does constrain his creative work in that way. And the evidence suggests that the universe has a rich biofriendly character, as if life was an important part of the plan.

What About Adam and Eve?

We make no claim that the description provided here is how God created us. Neither science nor the Bible answers that question. The Genesis account says little about how God created. Adam was created from dust and God's breath; Eve was created from Adam's rib; the animals, fish and birds were created by divine commands: "Let there be..." None of these "explanations" can possibly be actual descriptions. Human beings are mainly water, not dust, and there is no process by which an adult person can be made quickly from a rib. (Cloning would take thirty years and require technology that probably wasn't available in the Garden of Eden!) Based on what we know today about both science and the ancient world of the Hebrews, it is simply not reasonable to try to turn the brief comments in Genesis into a biologically accurate description of how humans originated. Our point is that the Genesis account does not tell us how God created—only that God did create and that human beings are a part of God's plan and not an accident.

In part because the Genesis account leaves the "how" question unanswered, there is room for scientific insights into how God created. The goal is that the two different viewpoints should not contradict each other; this requirement is, fortunately, easy to satisfy. But all the scientific evidence we have been discussing deals exclusively with the *physical* or *material* aspects of our creation. In order for this scientific picture to be fully integrated into a genuine and traditional Christian view, we must make appropriate connections at some level with the Genesis account and its allusions to the spiritual aspects of the first humans introduced there. Because the Genesis account is hermeneutically complex, it is not entirely clear exactly how this should be done, so what we offer here are simply some possibilities. We start with a brief survey of the most important features of the story.

The early chapters of Genesis introduce the reader to Adam and Eve, formed from the dust of the earth, brought to life by the breath of God (Genesis 2:7) and placed in a beautiful garden with a mysterious tree bearing fruit that gives knowledge. Adam and Eve are so blessed that God visits them in the evening.

God tells Adam and Eve that they can eat from any tree in the garden except the tree of the knowledge of good and evil. If they break this rule, God tells them that they will surely die (Genesis 2:16-17). Nonetheless, they disobey this command and are cursed and cast from the garden. God no longer visits them and even places an angel with a flaming sword at the entrance to the garden so they can't get back in.

This is the story of how Adam and Eve's relationship with God was broken. This breach, known as the Fall, marks not only the separation of God and humankind, but also the entry, in some sense, of evil into the world.

The familiar story of Adam and Eve is a staple of theological discourses, Sunday school lessons and the stained-glass motifs of Christianity's great cathedrals. This is the account that any evolutionary explanation for human origins must engage *constructively* if it is to be meaningfully Christian.

So how does this story fit into an evolutionary history where earth is billions of years old and humans originated hundreds of thousands of years ago in Africa? Is the story of Adam and Eve actual history or is something else going on here? Christians over the centuries have held many positions on this, ranging from straightforward literalist interpretations of the texts to readings that emphasize the theological content.[10]

Can a Literalist Reading Be Reconciled with Science?

Many Christians prior to the emergence of the historical science of geology in the eighteenth century interpreted the first chapters of Genesis as referring to actual places, people and events. In the medieval period, for example, adventurers traveled to the Middle East hunting for the Garden of Eden. Maps from this period even indicate where cartographers thought Eden was located and where Adam and Eve went after being expelled.[11] In the same way, the Institute for Creation Research and other contemporary groups have sent expeditions to Turkey searching for Noah's Ark.

Literalist readings of Genesis imply that God *specially* created Adam and Eve, and that all humans are descended from these original parents. Such readings, unfortunately, do not fit the evidence, for several reasons. First, there are two stories of creation, one in Genesis 1:1–2:3 and one in Genesis 2:4-25. These accounts have different chronological orders, a fact that didn't bother Christians who lived in the centuries before the discipline of history emerged, although it makes many Christians today uneasy. As odd as it sounds, people long ago talked about the past in radically different ways. Past events could be placed in an order reflecting their *importance,* for example, rather than their *chronology.* History is simply not done like this today, and we cannot imagine writing the history of the United States with the Civil War coming after World War II, just because the concerns of the Civil War seem to have more immediate relevance to us than those of World War II.

Literalist readings of Genesis run into historical trouble when we try to reconcile the chronological details of the different creation accounts in Genesis

1–2. Difficulties also arise when we work out the implications of the human race beginning with only two initial people. For example, there is the traditional problem of Cain's wife: where did she come from? The only possibility is that she was Cain's sister, but this conflicts with later biblical commands against incest. Even more problematic are the people Cain fears when he is banished from his homeland for killing his brother Abel. Genesis 4:13-14 says:

> Cain said to the Lord, "My punishment is more than I can bear! Today you are driving me from the land; and I will be hidden from your presence; I will be a restless wanderer on the earth, and whoever finds me will kill me."

It is implausible that the people trying to kill Cain are his extended family—siblings, nieces, nephews and so on—the text certainly does not suggest this. Along the same lines, Genesis mentions the city that Cain built and named after his son (Genesis 4:17). Who would populate this city or help build it?

Scientific evidence indicates a dramatically larger population at this point in history. Recently acquired genetic evidence also points to a population of several thousand people from whom all humans have descended, not just two. Finally, fossil and DNA records point strongly to a more unified creation reflected in the relatedness of humans and other animals.[12] The comparison of human and chimp chromosomes provides one of many compelling pieces of evidence for this unity, as we have seen earlier. We carry in our bodies this evidence of our relatedness to other species—evidence that argues strongly against a literalist interpretation of the Genesis creation account of humans.

What About a Nonliteral Interpretation, like the "Everyman Reading"?

The "everyman reading" of the creation story provides a different metaphorical take on the text that some would describe as more theologically liberal. This view understands the Fall as a story representing every human's individual rejection of God. The Fall was not a historical event but a statement of the common human condition that everyone agrees is deeply flawed and sinful. It does not matter in this interpretation if Adam and Eve were historical figures. Their deeds simply represent the actions of all humans and remind us of this troubling part of our natures.

This reading suggests that the story of Adam and Eve is the kind of traditional story that cultures use to understand themselves—stories that unpack the common experience of humanity. Such stories provide explanations for the culture's rituals, beliefs, worldview and so on. The story of the Fall provides an explanation for why all people seem to have a "dark side," and why it seems so much easier to be selfish than kind. It would be a story that mothers would tell to their children to explain why people did such terrible things to each other.

This interpretation is not popular, of course, among those who believe the Fall is a historical event. The apostle Paul, for example, compares Adam and Jesus in the book of Romans, describing Adam as a sort of representative of humanity who sinned and brought on the curse. Adam is contrasted with Jesus, the new representative, who brings life: "For if the many died by the trespass of the one man, how much more did God's grace and the gift that came by the grace of the one man, Jesus Christ, overflow to the many!" (Romans 5:15). Jesus, of course, is clearly a historical figure, and Paul seems to be referencing Jesus and Adam in the same way, thus suggesting that he thought of Adam as a historical figure.

Are There Other Nonliteral Readings?

Old Testament scholar Peter Enns offers the provocative thesis that "Adam is the beginning of Israel, not humanity." He notes a number of similarities between the story of Adam and the early history of Israel. Compare the following events with their obvious counterparts in the Garden of Eden:

1. The Israelites are given Canaan to inhabit, a lush land flowing with milk and honey.
2. They remain in the land as long as they obey the Mosaic law.
3. They persist in a pattern of disobedience and are exiled to

Babylon.

Enns suggests that "Israel's history happened first, and the Adam story was written to reflect that history. In other words, the Adam story is really an Israel story placed in primeval time. *It is not a story of human origins but of Israel's origins.*"

Enns suggests that these parallels are too remarkable to simply be a coincidence. He also notes that the word *adam* is ambiguous:

> Every commentator notes that sometimes "adam" represents *humanity* (so I will use the lower case); other times it is the name "Adam" (upper case) representing one *man.* What does this back and forth mean? It means that Adam is a special subset of adam.
>
> The character "Adam" is the focus of the story because he is the part of "adam" that God is really interested in. There is "adam" outside of Eden (in Nod), but inside of Eden, which is God's focus, there is only "Adam"—the one with which he has a unique relationship.
>
> The question in Genesis is whether "Adam" will be obedient to "the law" and stay in Eden, thus continuing this special relationship, or join the other "adam" outside in "exile." This is the same question with Israel: after being "created" by God, will they obey and remain in the land, or disobey and be exiled?

Enns concludes that the "Adam is Israel" interpretation is a "much better angle than seeing Adam as the first human and all humans are descended from him. Genesis does not support that reading."[13]

Are There Any Historical Views That Work with the Scientific Evidence?

A common synthetic view integrating the biblical and scientific accounts sees human-like creatures evolving as the scientific evidence indicates, steadily becoming more capable of relating to God. At a certain point in history, God entered into a special relationship with those who had developed the necessary characteristics, endowing them with the gift of his image. With this spiritual gift came the ability to know and experience evil—an opportunity grasped with tragic consequences that have carried through the history of our species.

Such scenarios are speculative, of course, but this view can fit whether the humans in question constitute a group—symbolized by Adam and Eve—or a specific male-female pair. In the case of a group, we can imagine God interacting with all members of the group and essentially initiating the relationship that exists today. If the initiative is with a single human couple, then that relationship would spread to and through their offspring as that subset of the existing population comes to dominate.[14]

In any event, the humans exercised their free will and caused the Fall. The mysterious connection of the Fall to the tree of knowledge of good and evil suggests that these humans exercised their moral consciousness by choosing to live independently, rather than by God's instruction. The Genesis narrative provides a vivid description of their consequent alienation from God.

These accounts fit with the genetic evidence of all species' relatedness and a larger initial population of humans. They also keep Adam—whether an individual or symbolizing a group—as representative of all humanity.

Are such views acceptable for a Christian? Many thoughtful, faithful Christians throughout history have subscribed to nonliteralist views of the Genesis accounts of creation. For example, C.S. Lewis held a similar view. In *The Problem of Pain,* Lewis describes the emergence of the image of God as follows:

> In the fullness of time, God caused to descend upon this organism, both on its psychology and physiology, a new kind of consciousness which could say "I" and "me," which could look upon itself as an object, which knew God, which could make judgments of truth, beauty and goodness, and which was so far above time that it could perceive time flowing past.[15]

Conclusion

The appeal of any of these scenarios for reconciling Genesis with the scientific account of our origins will depend on factors that are larger than our view of science or the Bible. The hermeneutically complex stories in Genesis do not explain themselves, nor do they offer any hints as to what approaches are most legitimate in dealing with science. We also emphasize that Christianity is centered on *Christ,* not on Adam and certainly not on any particular scientific theory. If our understanding of salvation through Christ requires only that we agree that humans are sinful and in need of salvation, then any of the discussed scenarios are adequate, including the "everyman reading." On the other hand, if we insist that our theology includes an account of how sin appeared in a sinless world, then we need historical connections to explain what happened.

The image of God is a further complicating factor. Christian thinkers have never been of one mind on this mysterious idea, although there is general agreement that it does not refer to our *physical* appearance, as if the word *image* is to be taken literally. If the image of God belongs exclusively to the human species, then there needs to be some sort of event where our species acquires it. On the other hand, perhaps the image of God is broader than simply our species, as one of us has argued.[16]

Such speculations are unlikely to converge on any simple historical model for how all this fits together. There will always be room for disagreement on this topic, just as there is on so many others. The various traditions within Christianity continue to have quite different ideas on everything from God's sovereignty to the propriety of female pastors and priests. We should not be surprised if differences on these questions remain as well.

We are encouraged, however, that the scientific evidence is compatible with various integrative scenarios, and even supportive in important ways.

9

The Grand Narrative of Creation

God saw all that he had made, and it was very good. And there was evening, and there was morning—the sixth day.

GENESIS 1:31

We close this book with a brief summary of the creative history of the universe, from the big bang to the big brain as some have put it. We do this to show the grandeur and awe-inspiring character of the story, countering claims from various constituencies that "God would not create in that way." All too often polemicists can make something attractive or unappealing based on the rhetoric used to describe it, rather than its true nature. Politics is the classic example. We have all seen how candidates running for office can smear each other until it seems nobody is worth voting for.

The scientific creation story has been described in a highly negative way by both young earth creationists and atheists alike. The creationists don't like it because it disagrees with a literal reading of the creation story in Genesis. So, too often they make it seem as *implausible* and un-Christian as possible. On the other hand, some atheists fashion the story into a club to bash religion and make it seem as *plausible* and un-Christian as possible. With both sides arguing that the scientific creation story is un-Christian, it is no wonder religious believers find it unattractive.

We would like to recast the scientific creation story to open up its grandeur, describing it as we see it—the unfolding creative work of God. To remind us that this is the story of creation we will intersperse the story with biblical references to the creation. Recognizing the sacred nature of the biblical text and our own profound limitations of understanding, we offer this story with humility and reverence. We hope, however, that our readers can catch a glimpse of the transcendent grandeur that brings this story to life.

The Modern Creation Story

In the beginning God created the heavens and the earth.

The universe begins with a mystery called, for lack of a better term (and there once was a contest to find a better term), the "big bang." The moment of the big bang is beyond the grasp of science. We cannot observe it directly; our theories take us close to that moment but stop short, and our simulations of the early universe in laboratory settings can't get back to that point. What we can do, though, is see the results, and our simulations and theories start working just a fraction of a second after that moment of creation.

What appears at the big bang is what we might call the rational foundations—or the *logos*—of the universe. The deepest and most fundamental laws of physics, with their various properties, emerge. These laws specify the kinds of physical interactions that can take place. Remarkably, as we saw in chapter seven, there are only four kinds of interactions that occur in nature: gravitational, electromagnetic, strong nuclear and weak nuclear. Every event, from the thoughts in our head as we read these words, to the laughter of a toddler, to the light being produced by the sun, rests on these four interactions.

Out of the big bang comes a specification that there will be only two kinds of physical objects in the world: quarks and leptons, and their mirror-image antiparticles. Protons and neutrons are composed of quarks; the electron is the best-known example of a lepton. Every physical object, from a potato chip to the Eiffel Tower to the diamond on an engagement ring, is made from quarks and leptons.

All the natural phenomena that generate the grand narrative of the universe, no matter how rich or mundane, result from quarks and leptons interacting via four kinds of interactions. Who could possibly guess that a world defined so simply could become so interesting?

The four forces and two particles in the universe initially seem like nothing more than chaotic parts of an incomprehensibly messy maelstrom. But then things start to happen—things that no team of scientists or even science-fiction writers could have imagined, much less predicted. Out of what looks like chaos comes a most remarkable and transcendent order.

> In the beginning was the Word, and the Word was with God, and the Word was God.

The quarks, with electrical charges of 2/3 and −1/3, combine under the influence of the strong nuclear force, and soon they are all gathered into protons and neutrons, which have electrical charges of 1 and 0.

The protons, neutrons and electrons buzz about as the universe expands and cools. As the temperature declines, the electrons drop into orbits around the protons to make hydrogen atoms—unimaginable numbers of hydrogen atoms spread across the entire universe.

All the particles in the universe are now electrically neutral; it turns out the universe has a perfect balance between the positive and negative charges. Once the particles in the universe have become atoms, with no net charge on them, the electrical force becomes far less relevant and the weaker gravitational force takes over. The hydrogen atoms are gathered by gravity into huge clusters, steadily growing until much of the hydrogen in the universe is gathered into gigantic clouds. The clouds get steadily larger in size, surpassing the size of the moon, then the earth, then large planets like Jupiter.

> And God said, "Let there be lights in the expanse of the sky to separate the day from the

> night, and let them serve as signs to mark seasons and days and years, and let them be lights in the expanse of the sky to give light on the earth."

At a critical point the gigantic clouds of hydrogen ignite. Across the universe great clouds of hydrogen turn into stars; gravity has made them so dense that the atoms are crushed together until they start to fuse. Here we discover one of the many remarkable balances in nature: the strong force cooperates intimately with this gravitational crushing, and the hydrogen atoms combine to become helium atoms. The process that generates starlight also builds the periodic table—multitasking on a cosmic scale—as the simplest atoms, hydrogen, fuse to make helium. The fusion process continues to build increasingly heavier atoms: lithium, beryllium, boron and then the all-important carbon. And on to nitrogen, oxygen, neon, sodium and beyond.

Some of the largest stars become overwhelmed by their own gravity and undergo catastrophic inward collapses so violent that the stars actually bounce and explode with the force of a billion atomic bombs. Such explosions populate vast regions of space with the elements created inside the star; the explosions are strangely orderly and eerily silent since there is no sound in space. Gravity gathers the stellar material back into big clouds again. A large cloud at the center of the explosion can become another, second-generation, star.

> The earth was formless and empty, darkness was over the surface of the deep, and the Spirit of God was hovering over the waters.

The smaller clouds, with their rich roster of elements fused from hydrogen, gradually compress into balls orbiting about the second-generation star. Many of these smaller balls, which will one day be called planets, have a remarkable new kind of structure formed from chemical combinations of atoms. One interesting molecular combination is of hydrogen and oxygen, and is known as H[2] O. In most parts of the universe, this molecule is solid, in the form of ice. In other parts the H[2] O is a gas. But on planets exactly the right distance from a star, the H[2] O is liquid, a particular liquid called water.

Very complex structures, from a mechanical point of view, have been built from simple raw materials; a universe that was once nothing but vast swaths of hydrogen gas now has solar systems where chemically rich planets orbit about stars with remarkably stable outputs of light. Planets at just the right distance from their "suns" have the right temperature for liquid H[2] O. This water is surprisingly capable of encouraging the formation of ever more complex molecules like amino acids, carbohydrates and lipids. By providing a medium in which atoms and molecules can jostle around gently, various combinations can form naturally. The result is increasing complexity.

> And God said, "Let the land produce living creatures according to their kinds: livestock,

> creatures that move along the ground, and wild animals, each according to its kind."

These complex materials grow ever more varied until one particular arrangement actually starts duplicating itself. The ability of this structure to make copies of itself from the surrounding materials enables it to dominate the local environment and soon the waters are filled with this new process. The universe has come to life. In some extraordinary sense we can now speak in meaningful terms about the universe having *information*—tiny blueprints that direct the formation of ever more interesting and varied forms of simple life.

Subtle interactions between these primitive life forms as they compete for resources make them increasingly more robust as the stronger ones reproduce themselves more effectively. The copying process, driven by a surprisingly creative set of molecular interactions, steadily and mysteriously pushes the life forms to ever greater complexity. The information molecule driving all this will one day be identified as DNA, which will be discovered to have an amazing ability to both reliably make copies of itself and to explore small variations. These explorations will allow the molecule to locate small improvements to its basic structure and then reproduce that new variation with greater efficiency until it would come to dominate.

A major change occurs when single-celled forms of life began to cooperate and form multicelled organisms. This cooperation empowers entirely new developments that will lead to astonishing increases in complexity and sophistication. Eventually specialized functions will emerge, enabling organisms to collect visual information, to hear sounds, to have body temperatures that are constant, to have solid skeletal structures that provide enormous protection when they are on the outside and great mechanical dexterity when they are on the inside.

> Then God said, "Let us make man in our image, in our likeness, and let them rule over the fish of the sea and the birds of the air, over the livestock, over all the earth, and over all the creatures that move along the ground."

As complexity increases, the need to process more and more information from the external world increases also, and a remarkable central processing unit of enormous power and sophistication emerges. These *brains,* as they would one day be called, endow their possessors with a growing capacity to function in and to understand the world.

Mysteriously these brains that evolve in response to challenges having to do with survival and reproduction acquire capacities to think about complex subjects. The capacity to do mathematics emerges and with it comes increasingly deep insights into the patterns and underlying order of creation.

Eventually the most advanced of the life forms on the planet, human beings, become deeply religious. Throughout the history of our species belief in God or gods has been close to universal. Abstractions like right and wrong, the meaning of life, and where everything came from have become critically important questions. The religious impulse developed into one of the deepest aspects of our complicated understanding of ourselves.

And God saw that it was good.

Annotated Bibliography

This volume covers a lot of ground, much of which is covered in different ways by both the present authors and other scholars working in this field. Furthermore, every chapter surveys topics that have received book-length treatments from other scholars. We offer, in this short bibliographic essay, a survey of references that are recommended for further study.

A natural place to start is the website BioLogos.org, where this project began. This website has a variety of resources, from succinct essays on frequently asked questions to scholarly papers and daily blogs from leaders in this field.

To pursue the topics of this book in more depth, we refer readers to our books *The Language of God: A Scientist Presents Evidence for Belief* by Francis Collins, and *Saving Darwin: How to Be a Christian and Believe in Evolution* by Karl Giberson, both of which offer overviews, at a popular level, as well as personal reflections on how we think about this topic. We also strongly recommend *Coming to Peace with Science: Bridging the Worlds Between Faith and Biology* by Darrel Falk, the president of BioLogos. *Creation or Evolution: Do We Have to Choose?* by the Catholic British biologist Denis Alexander and *Evolutionary Creation: A Christian Approach to Evolution* by the Baptist Canadian biologist and biblical scholar Denis Lamoureux provide in-depth overviews. Virtually all of their insights are useful to Christians from any tradition. The latter is available in an abbreviated volume with the unusual title *I Love Jesus and I Accept Evolution.* Pastor Daniel Harrel's *Nature's Witness: How Evolution Can Inspire Faith* provides an accessible overview from a conservative evangelical perspective. *Origins: A Reformed Look at Creation, Design and Evolution* by Calvin College professors (and spouses) Deborah Haarsma and Loren Haarsma provides an excellent introduction that has been used in Christian high schools.

The prolific agnostic Michael Ruse has given this topic a full treatment in *Can a Darwinian Be a Christian?* Fair and balanced, this volume defends the compatibility of evolution and faith. Ruse's many volumes on this topic are useful for further study, especially as he writes without hostility to religion.

For an overview of the different positions at play in this controversy, the place to start is *Species of Origins: America's Search for a Creation Story* by Karl Giberson and Donald Yerxa, the only book that examines all the major positions from a position of nonadvocacy. *Three Views on Creation and Evolution,* edited by J.P. Moreland and John Mark Reynolds, presents young and old earth creationism, and theistic evolution by some of their leading proponents. In-depth responses provide helpful clarifications.

Any overview of young earth creationism should start with *Scientific Creationism* by Henry Morris that, although dated, is a most important and influential volume. Ken Ham's *The Lie: Evolution* outlines the approach of America's most influential young earth creationist. An abundance of information from this perspective can be found on Ken Ham's Answers in Genesis website (www.answersingenesis.org).

Many of the issues covered in this book relate to biblical interpretation, and the already-mentioned books by Lamoureux and Alexander address these issues in some detail. There are also many resources that deal specifically with the ancient context of the Old Testament and how that context affects our understanding of the Bible. An excellent and accessible book by a conservative evangelical Old Testament scholar is *The Lost World of Genesis One* by John Walton, who teaches at Wheaton College. A good, if more demanding, discussion of the nature of biblical inspiration can be found in *Inspiration and Incarnation: Evangelicals and the Problem of the Old Testament* by BioLogos senior fellow in biblical studies Peter Enns. Also demanding is Richard Middleton's *The Liberating Image,* which focuses on the image of God in Genesis 1 and how Israel's view is very different from other ancient religions. An excellent and highly accessible look at reading Genesis in its ancient context as well as from a theological point of view is *How to Read Genesis* by Tremper Longman III.

For presentations of intelligent design by its leading proponents we suggest starting with Stephen Meyer's *The Signature in the Cell: DNA and the Evidence for Intelligent Design,* Michael Behe's

Darwin's Black Box: The Biochemical Challenge to Evolution and *The Edge of Evolution: The Search for the Limits of Darwinism,* and William Dembski's *Intelligent Design: The Bridge Between Science and Theology.* Phillip Johnson's *Darwin on Trial* launched the intelligent design movement and is written in a lively and compelling style. The anthology *Mere Creation,* edited by William Dembski, provides a helpful and wide-ranging collection of essays on intelligent design.

The various hypotheses proposed under the intelligent design umbrella have been controversial and generated extensive responses. Two of the best are by the Brown University biologist and active Catholic Ken Miller: *Finding Darwin's God: A Scientist's Search for Common Ground Between God and Evolution* and *Only a Theory: Evolution and the Battle for America's Soul.* A balanced and wide-ranging critique can also be found in philosopher Robert Pennock's *Tower of Babel: The Evidence Against the New Creationism.*

Robert Stewart has edited a volume we can also recommend for an engaging dialogue: *Intelligent Design: William A. Dembski and Michael Ruse in Dialogue.* Ruse and Dembski are on completely opposite sides of this question, but they are friends, and this dialogue never gets personal.

Because so much of this controversy is shaped by its history, we recommend that interested readers look at *Evolution: History of an Idea* by Ed Larson. We can also recommend Larson's Pulitzer Prize–winning *Summer for the Gods: The Scopes Trial and America's Continuing Debate Over Science and Religion.* The definitive history of the creation movement is *The Creationists: From Scientific Creationism to Intelligent Design* by Ronald Numbers.

Biographies of Darwin are also valuable as history, and there are a remarkable number of outstanding and very readable accounts to choose from. *Darwin: The Life of a Tormented Evolutionist* by Adrian Desmond and James Moore is one of the best. They have also produced a remarkable sequel focusing on Darwin's enthusiastic abolitionism: *Darwin's Sacred Cause: How Hatred of Slavery Shaped Darwin's Views on Evolution.* Readers interested in a shorter biography of Darwin should look at Randall Keynes's *Darwin, His Daughter, and Human Evolution.* This very readable volume was the basis for the movie *The Creation* starring Paul Bettany as Charles Darwin and Jennifer Connolly as his remarkable wife Emma.

For readers interested in the nature and history of the cosmos, including the fascinating design argument, we recommend theologian Alister McGrath's *A Fine-Tuned Universe: The Quest for God in Science and Theology.* Paul Davies's *Cosmic Jackpot: Why OurUniverse Is Just Right for Life* is a readable treatment of the same topic from an author who takes the idea of God seriously but is not a Christian.

We look forward to continuing the conversation with you. Join us at www.biologos.org.

Notes

Introduction

[1] Carl Gustav Boberg, "How Great Thou Art" (1885) <www.greatchristianhymns.com/how-great-thou-art.html>.

[2] "Discrete Genes Are Inherited: Gregor Mendel," *Understanding Evolution,* University of California Museum of Paleontology <http://evolution.berkeley.edu/evolibrary/article/_0_0/history_1320>.

[3] Michael Ruse, *Can a Darwinian Be a Christian: The Relationship Between Science and Religion* (Cambridge: Cambridge University Press, 2001); and Daniel Harrell, *Nature's Witness: How Evolution Can Inspire Faith* (Nashville: Abingdon, 2008).

[4] Richard Weikert, *From Darwin to Hitler* (New York: Palgrave Macmillan, 2004). See also William Dembski, "What's Wrong with Uttering 'Darwin' and 'Hitler' in the Same Breath?" *Uncommon Descent,* April 18, 2008 <www.uncommondescent.com/evolution/some-of-my-favorite-quotes-by-darwinists>.

[5] Francis Galton, *Memories of My Life* (New York: E.P. Dutton, 1909), p.323.

[6] Harry Hamilton Laughlin, *Eugenical Sterilization in the United States* (Chicago: Psychopathic Laboratory of the Municipal Court of Chicago, 1922).

[7] Ibid.
[8] Steven Jay Gould, "Chapter 20: Carrie Buck's Daughter," in *The Flamingo's Smile* (New York: W.W. Norton, 1985), pp.206-318.
[9] "Eugenics," *Encyclopedia Britannica Online,* 2010 <www.britannica.com/EBchecked/topic/195069/eugenics>.
[10] Charles Darwin, *The Descent of Man, and Selection in Relation to Sex* (London: J. Murray, 1871), 1:168. Available online at John van Wyhe, ed., The Complete Work of Charles Darwin Online (2002-2010) <http://darwin-online.org.uk>. A similarly misleading quote is used in *Expelled: No Intelligence Allowed* (Rampant Films, 2008).
[11] Jeffrey P. Schloss, "The Expelled Controversy: Overcoming or Raising Walls of Division?" *American Scientific Affiliation* (2008) <www.asa3.org/ASA/resources/Schloss200805.pdf>.
[12] Darwin, *Descent of Man,* pp.168-69.
[13] Schloss, "The Expelled Controversy."
[14] Ibid.
[15] Adrian Desmond and James Moore, *Darwin's Sacred Cause* (New York: Houghton Mifflin Harcourt, 2009). See also the first chapter of *Darwin's Sacred Cause* at Adrian Desmond and James Moore, "First Chapters," *New York Times,* January 30, 2009 <www.nytimes.com/2009/02/01/books/chapters/chapter-darwins-sacred-cause.html>.

Chapter 1: Do I Have to Believe in Evolution?

[1] Brannon House, "Christian Worldview for Students," Worldview Weekend 2006, Collierville, Tenn., p.65.

[2] Ibid., p.66.

[3] Homepage, A Scientific Dissent from Darwinism <www.dissentfromdarwin.org>.

[4] "Project Steve," National Center for Science Education, October 17, 2008 <http://ncse.com/taking-action/project-steve>.

[5] In general, the definition of a species is a group of individuals that are capable of interbreeding and producing fertile offspring. However, it is difficult to apply this definition to the earliest stages of microbial life on earth, since there appears to have been extensive horizontal gene transfer between different early organisms.

[6] "Discrete Genes Are Inherited: Gregor Mendel," *Understanding Evolution,* University of California Museum of Paleontology <http://evolution.berkeley.edu/evolibrary/article/_0/history_13>.

[7] "Theodosius Dobzhansky," UXL Encyclopedia of World Biography, *FindArticles.com,* November 24, 2009 <http://findarticles.com/p/articles/mi_gx5229/is_2003/ai_n19146093>.

[8] Benjamin B. Warfield, "Evolution or Development," in *Evolutions, Scripture and Science: Selected Writings,* ed. Mark A. Noll and David N. Livingstone (Grand Rapids: Baker, 2000), p.130.

[9] Henry Morris, "The Vanishing Case for Evolution," Institute for Creation Research <www.icr.org/index.php?module=articles&action=view&ID=260>.

[10] Jonathan Weiner, *The Beak of the Finch: A Story of Evolution in Our Time* (New York: Alfred Knopf, 1994). For a more detailed response to these claims, see Francis S. Collins, *The Language of God: A Scientist Presents Evidence for Belief* (New York: Free Press, 2006), p.132. See also Darrel R. Falk, *Coming to Peace with Science: Bridging the Worlds Between Faith and Biology* (Downers Grove, Ill.: InterVarsity Press, 2004), p.130.

[11] Falk, *Coming to Peace with Science,* p.131.

[12] Ken Ham, *The Lie: Evolution* (El Cajon, Calif.: Creation-Life, 1987), p.26.

[13] Timothy Ferris, *Coming of Age in the Milky Way* (New York: Morrow, 1988).

Chapter 2: Can We Really Know the Earth Is Billions of Years Old?

[1] G. Brent Dalrymple, *The Age of the Earth* (Stanford, Calif.: Stanford University Press, 1991), p.191.

[2] "Origin of Human Life," Pollingreport.com, 2010 <www.pollingreport.com/science.htm>.

[3] Karl W. Giberson, *Worlds Apart: The Unholy War Between Religion and Science* (Kansas City: Beacon Hill, 1993), pp.146-54.

[4] See, for example, John Walton, *The Lost World of Genesis One: Ancient Cosmology and the Origins Debate* (Downers Grove, Ill.: InterVarsity Press, 2009).

[5] Darrel R. Falk, *Coming to Peace with Science* (Downers Grove, Ill.: InterVarsity Press, 2004), pp.79-80.

[6] Ken Ham et al., *The Answers Book* (El Cajon, Calif.: Master Books, 1991), pp.192-94.

[7] Barry Setterfield and Trevor Norman, "Atomic Constants, Light, and Time," Genesis Science Research, August 1987 <www.setterfield.org/report/report.html>.

[8] "Arguments That Should Never Be Used," Answers in Genesis (2010) <www.answersingenesis.org/get-answers/topic/arguments-we-dont-use>.

[9] Hugh Ross, *The Creator and the Cosmos: How the Greatest Scientific Discoveries of the Century Reveal God* (Colorado Springs: NavPress, 1993). See also William Lane Craig, "The Ultimate Question of Origins: God and the Beginning of the Universe," Reasonable Faith with William Lane Craig (1999) <www.reasonablefaith.org/site/News2?page=NewsArticle&id=5180>.

[10] "Hubble Uncovers Oldest 'Clocks' in Space to Read Age of Universe," HubbleSite, April 24, 2002 <http://hubblesite.org/newscenter/archive/releases/2002/10>.

[11] Ibid.

[12] Based on example in Falk, *Coming to Peace with Science,* pp.77-78. For discussion on determining the actual brightness of stars, see W.L. Freedman, "The Expansion Rate of the Universe," *Scientific American* 267, no.5 (1992):54.

[13] Two further methods confirm the result of an ancient universe. In 2002 the Hubble telescope discovered white dwarf stars that also pointed to an ancient universe. These dying stars grow increasingly faint with time, allowing them to be used as "clocks" by measuring their brightness. These discovered white dwarfs were found to be 12-13 billion years old, which, combined with an earlier finding that they formed ~1 billion years after the big bang, also pointed to a universe 13-14 billion years old. In 2003 astronomers were able to map cosmic background radiation, leftover heat from the big bang, which emitted a faint glow at 2.725 K (-270°C), as noted in Paul Davies, *Cosmic Jackpot: Why Our Universe Is Just Right for Life* (London: Penguin Press, 2006). Studying its distribution, they were able to calculate the more precise age of 13.7 billion years, as ex-

plained in Bob White, "The Age of the Earth," *Faraday Papers* no.8 (2007) <www.st-edmunds.cam.ac.uk/faraday/Papers.php>.

[14] The ages of the dead trees were calibrated by comparing rings from the end of their lives to the early rings of trees still living. For example, a tree from 11,800 years ago lived 6,000 years and then died. Its last 200 rings can be calibrated with the first 200 rings of a living tree that is currently 6,000 years old (Falk, *Coming to Peace with Science,* p.73).

[15] There are actually even older sediment layers, but beyond 35,000 years layers become so compressed that they cannot be distinguished for accurate dating (ibid., p.74).

[16] Roger C. Wiens, "Radiometric Dating: A Christian Perspective," American Scientific Affiliation, 2002 <www.asa3.org/aSA/resources/wiens2002.pdf>. See also North Greenland Ice Core Project Members, "High-Resolution Record of Northern Hemisphere Climate Extending into the Last Interglacial Period," *Nature* 431 (2004):147-51, which reports ages back to 123,000 years. On glacial ice, see EPICA Community Members, "Eight Glacial Cycles from an Antarctic Ice Core," *Nature* 429 (2004):623-28.

[17] Here is a more detailed description from White's paper: "Perhaps more surprisingly,

changes in the Earth's orbit cause long-term cyclicity in climate patterns, known as Milankovitch cycles. Eccentricity of the Earth's orbit round the sun produces 100,000 and 413,000 year cycles, tilt of the Earth's axis generates 40,000 year cyclicity, and precession of the Earth's axis of rotation creates cycles at approximately 19,000 and 23,000 years. Identification of these cycles by their rhythmic climatic effect on ancient sediments allows precision dating back to 30 million years" (White, "Age of the Earth," p.2).

[18] White, "The Age of the Earth." Here is a more detailed description from Bob White's paper: "A final example of irregular cyclic changes that can be used to date rocks is their magnetic polarity. Fluid motions in the Earth's liquid outer core create a dynamo, which generates a global dipole magnetic field roughly aligned with the Earth's axis of rotation. The magnetic field reverses its polarity on average 2-3 times per million years. Since rocks bearing magnetized minerals record the direction of the magnetic field at the time they were deposited, the polarity reversals can be recognized and used to date the volcanic basement of the seafloor back 170 million years. This technique was the basis of recognizing seafloor spreading, leading quickly to the plate tectonics theory

which in the 1960s revolutionized geological interpretation of the Earth's history" (ibid., p.2).

[19] Wiens, "Radiometric Dating," p.13.

[20] White, "Age of the Earth," p.4.

[21] Robert Schadewald, "The 1998 International Conference on Creationism," *National Center for Science Education* 18, issue 3 (1998):22-25, 33 <http://ncse.com/rncse/18/3/1998-international-conference-creationism>. See also Paul A. Nelson and John Mark Reynolds, *Young Earth Creationism* (Grand Rapids: Zondervan, 1999), p.51.

[22] Henry Morris and John Morris, *The Modern Creation Trilogy,* vol.1, *Science and Creation* (Green Forest, Ark.: Master Books, 1996), p.76.

[23] See Ron Numbers, *The Creationists* (Los Angeles: University of California Press, 1993), pp.184-213.

[24] Origen *First Principles* 4.3, trans. G. Butterworth (London: SPCK, 1936), quoted in Ernest Lucas, "Interpreting Genesis in the 21st Century," *Faraday Papers,* no.11 (2007) <www.st-edmunds.cam.ac.uk/faraday/resources/Faraday%20Papers/Faraday%20Paper%2011%20Lucas_EN.pdf>. Also available at "De Principiis (Book IV)," New Advent (2009) <www.newadvent.org/fathers/04124.htm>.

[25] Gillian Clark, *Augustine: The Confessions,* Landmarks of World Literature (New York: Cambridge University Press, 1993).

[26] Augustine, De Genesi ad litteram, 1.14.28, trans. J.H. Taylor, *St. Augustine: The Literal Meaning of Genesis,* Ancient Christian Writers 41 (New York: Newman Press, 1982).

[27] For a further discussion of Augustine's perspective on creation, see chapters eight and fifteen of Alister McGrath, *A Finely Tuned Universe: The Quest for God in Science and Theology* (Louisville: Westminster John Knox Press, 2009).

[28] William E. Carroll, "Aquinas and the Big Bang," *First Things* 97 (1999):18-20.

[29] Thomas Aquinas, "Question 74: All the Seven Days in Common," in *The Summa Theologica of St. Thomas Aquinas,* trans. Fathers of the English Dominican Province, 2nd ed. (London: Burns Oates & Washbourne, 1920). Also available online at "Summa Theologica," New Advent (2008) <www.newadvent.org/summa/1074.htm#2>.

[30] John Wesley, *Wesley's Notes on the Bible* (Grand Rapids: Francis Asbury Press, 1987), p.22. Also available online at John Wesley, "John Wesley's Notes on the Bible," Wesley Center Online (2007) <http://wesley.nnu.edu/john_wesley/notes/index.htm>.

[31] John Wesley, *A Survey of the Wisdom of God in the Creation: Or, a Compendium of Natural Philosophy,* 3rd ed. (London: J. Fry, 1777), 2:463.

[32] The Catholic Church also acknowledges the diversity of early Christian interpretations of Genesis. See, for example, "Creation and Genesis," Catholic Answers <www.catholic.com/library/Creation_and_Genesis.asp>.

[33] Ronald L. Numbers, *The Creationists: From Scientific Creationism to Intelligent Design* (Cambridge, Mass.: Harvard University Press, 2006), p.214.

[34] Augustine, *The Literal Meaning of Genesis* (Hyde Park, N.Y.: New York Press, 2002), cited in Alister E. McGrath, *The Foundations of Dialogue in Science and Religion* (Oxford: Blackwell, 1998), p.119.

[35] José de Acosta, *The Natural and Moral History of the Indies,* Natural History 1-4 (New York: Lenox Hill, 1970), p.23.

Chapter 3: How Do We Relate Science and Religion?

[1] Stephen J. Gould, "Nonoverlapping Magisteria," *Natural History* 106 (1997):16-22. See also Stephen Jay Gould, *Rocks of Ages: Science and Religion in the Fullness of Life* (New York: Ballantine Books, 1999), p.88.

[2] John Hedley Brooke, *Science and Religion: Some Historical Perspectives* (Cambridge: Cambridge University Press, 1991).

[3] Arthur Eddington, cited in Francis S. Collins, *The Language of God: A Scientist Presents Evidence for Belief* (New York: Free Press, 2006), p.229. See also Arthur Stanley Eddington, *The Philosophy of Physical Science* (New York: Macmillan, 1939).

[4] Rodney Stark, *For the Glory of God: How Monotheism Led to Reformations, Science, Witch-Hunts, and the End of Slavery* (Princeton, N.J.: Princeton University Press, 2003), pp.160-63.

[5] Roger Trigg, "Does Science Need Religion?" *Faraday Papers,* no.2 (April 2007) <www.st-edmunds.cam.ac.uk/faraday/Papers.php>. See also John Hedley Brooke, *Science and Religion: Some Historical Perspectives* (New York: Cambridge University Press, 1991).

[6] Alfred North Whitehead, *Science and the Modern World* (New York: Free Press, 1967), p.13.

[7] See, for example, the appendix to Collins, *Language of God,* p.235.

[8] Galileo Galilei, *Discoveries and Opinions of Galileo: Including The Starry Messenger* (1610), *Letter to the Grand Duchess Christina* (1615), *Excerpts from Letters on Sunspots* (1613), *and The Assayer* (1623), trans. Stillman Drake (New York: Anchor Books, 1990), p.186.

[9] Donald MacKay, *The Open Mind, and Other Essays* (Leicester, U.K.: Inter-Varsity Press, 1988), pp.151-52, quoted in Ernest Lucas, "Interpreting Genesis in the 21st Century," *Faraday Papers,* no.11 (April 2007) <www.st-edmunds.cam.ac.uk/faraday/Papers.php>.

[10] We should point out that the biblical authors had no concept of the earth as a planet. The Hebrew word for "earth" was the word for "land" or "soil," not "planet."

[11] William R. Shea and Mariano Artigas, *Galileo in Rome* (New York: Oxford University Press, 2003).

[12] Peter Enns, "'Hey, Get Away from My Bible!' Christian Appropriation of a Jewish Bible," *A Time to Tear Down A Time to Build*<http://peterennsonline.com/articles-and-essays/"hey-get-away-from-my-bible"-christian-appro priation-of-a-jewish-bible>.

[13] C.S. Lewis, *An Experiment in Criticism* (Cambridge: Cambridge University Press, 1961), p.19.

[14] Lucas, "Interpreting Genesis in the 21st Century."

[15] Ibid., p.2.

[16] Abraham Mitrie Rihbany, *The Syrian Christ* (Boston: Houghton Mifflin, 1916), pp.131-32.

[17] Jonathan Went, "Biblical Hebrew" (2003) <www.biblicalhebrew.com/nt/camelneedle.htm>.

[18] Rory C. Foster, *Studies in the Life of Christ: Introduction, the Early Period, the Middle Period, the Final Week* (Joplin, Mo.: College Press, 1995), p.1387.

[19] Bernard Ramm, *Protestant Biblical Interpretation: A Textbook of Hermeneutics,* 3rd ed. (Grand Rapids: Baker, 1970), p.11.

[20] J. C. Polkinghorne, *Science and the Trinity: The Christian Encounter with Reality* (New Haven, Conn.: Yale University Press, 2006), p.44.

[21] Lucas, "Interpreting Genesis in the 21st Century," p.3.

[22] Kenneth E. Bailey, *The Cross and the Prodigal: Luke 15 Through the Eyes of Middle Eastern Peasants* (Downers Grove, Ill.: InterVarsity Press, 2005), pp.66-74.

[23] Lucas, "Interpreting Genesis in the 21st Century," pp.3-4.

[24] Ibid., p.2.

[25] Karen Strand Winslow, "Understanding Earth," Science and the Sacred, September 25, 2009 <http://blog.beliefnet.com/scienceandthesacred/2009/09/understanding-earth.html>.

[26] Lucas, "Interpreting Genesis in the 21st Century," p.1.

Chapter 4: Can Scientific and Scriptural Truth Be Reconciled?

[1] John Polkinghorne, "Is Science Enough?" *Sewanee Theological Review* 39, no.1 (1995):11-26 <www.sewanee.edu/theology/str/strpapers.html#Polkinghorne>.

[2] Ibid. Please also note that this response assumes that the individual has free will.

[3] See Colin Humphreys, "The Star of Bethlehem," *Science and Christian Belief* 5 (1995):83-101.

[4] John Polkinghorne, "The Science and Religion Debate: An Introduction," *Faraday Papers,* no.1 (April 2007) <www.st-edmunds.cam.ac.uk/faraday/Papers.php>.

[5] John D. Barrow, *The Constants of Nature: From Alpha to Omega—The Numbers That Encode the Deepest Secrets of the Universe* (New York: Pantheon Books, 2002).

[6] Stephen Jay Gould, *The Mismeasure of Man* (New York: W.W. Norton, 1996).

[7] Richard Harter, "Piltdown Man," Talk Origins Archive, October 30, 2006 <http://home.tiac.net/~cri_a/piltdown/piltdown.html>.

[8] Roger Trigg, "Does Science Need Religion?" *Faraday Papers,* no.2 (April 2007) <www.st-edmunds.cam.ac.uk/faraday/Papers.php>.

[9] Ibid.

[10] bFrancis Bacon, *The Advancement of Learning; Colours of Good and Evil; The Essays* (London: Adamant Media, 2005).

[11] David N. Livingstone, *Darwin's Forgotten Defenders: The Encounter Between Evangelical Theology and Evolutionary Thought* (Grand Rapids: Eerdmans, 1987), p.118.

[12] A. H. Strong, quoted in Livingstone, *Darwin's Forgotten Defenders* (Vancouver, B.C.: Regent College Publishing, 1987), p.129.

[13] Francis S. Collins, *The Language of God: A Scientist Presents Evidence for Belief* (New York: Free Press, 2006), p.200. John C. Polkinghorne, *Science and Providence: God's Interaction with the World* (Philadelphia: Templeton Foundation Press, 2005), p.11.

[15] Ibid., p.7.

[16] Darrel R. Falk, *Coming to Peace with Science: Bridging the Worlds Between Faith and Biology* (Downers Grove, Ill.: InterVarsity Press, 2004), pp.101-3.

Chapter 5: Science and the Existence of God

[1] G. K. Chesterton, *Twelve Types* (Middlesex, U.K.: Echo Library, 2008), p.27.

[2] Francis S. Collins, *The Language of God: A Scientist Presents Evidence for Belief* (New York: Free Press, 2006), p.43.

[3] Charles Darwin, quoted in Michael Ruse, *Darwin and Design* (Cambridge, Mass.: Harvard University Press, 2003), p.127.

[4] William Dembski, *The End of Christianity: Finding a Good God in an Evil World* (Nashville: B & H Publishing, 2009), pp.142-55.

[5] Darrel Falk, "On Reducing Irreducible Complexity, Part II," Science and the Sacred, September 21, 2009 <http://blog.beliefnet.com/scienceandthesacred/author/darrel-falk-1/2009/09/index.html>.

[6] Karl W. Giberson, "Evolution and the Problem of Evil," Science and the Sacred, September 28, 2009 <http://blog.beliefnet.com/scienceandthesacred/author/karl-giberson-1/2009/09/index.html>.

[7] William Dembski, "Darrel Falk's Misshapen Theology of Evolution," Uncommon Descent, September 22, 2009 <www.uncommondescent.com/intelligent-design/darrell-falks-misshapen-theology-of-evolution>.

[8] Ibid.

[9] Martin Gardner, *The Whys of a Philosophical Scrivener* (New York: William Morrow, 1999).

[10] Frederick Robert Tennant, quoted in ibid.

[11] Leibniz made his classic argument in his 1710 work *Essais de Théodicée sur la bonté de Dieu, la liberté de l'homme et l'origine du mal* (or *Essays on the Justice of God and the Freedom of Man in the Origin of Evil).*

[12] John C. Polkinghorne, *The Faith of a Physicist: Reflections of a Bottom-Up Thinker* (Princeton, N.J.: Princeton University Press, 1996), p.83.

[13] See, for example, Greg Epstein, *Good Without God: What a Billion Non-Religious People Believe* (New York: William Morrow, 2009).

[14] John Polkinghorne, *Belief in God in an Age of Science* (New Haven, Conn.: Yale University Press, 1998). See also Tim Keller, *The Reason for God* (New York: Penguin Group, 2008).

[15] William Paley, *Natural Theology* (Cary, N.C.: Oxford University Press, 2006), p.7.

[16] Richard Dawkins, *The Blind Watchmaker* (New York: W.W. Norton, 1987), p.6.

[17] Robert Wright, *The Evolution of God* (New York: Little, Brown, 2009).

[18] James Franklin, *What Science Knows and How It Knows It* (New York: Encounter Books, 2009), pp.249-50.

[19] Stephen Hawking, *A Brief History of Time* (New York: Bantam Books, 1988).

[20] Clark Pinnock et al., *The Openness of God: A Biblical Challenge to the Traditional Understanding of God* (Downers Grove, Ill.: Inter-Varsity Press, 1994); Gregory Boyd, *God of the Possible: A Biblical Introduction to the Open View of God* (Grand Rapids: Baker, 2007).

[21] Lee Smolin, *The Life of the Cosmos* (New York: Oxford University Press, 1999).

[22] Bertrand Russell, *Why I Am Not a Christian, and Other Essays on Religion and Related Subjects,* ed. George Allen (New York: Simon & Schuster, 1957), p.107.

Chapter 6: Why Is Darwin's Theory So Controversial?

[1] The story of the wise men (Matthew 2:1-12) does not specify their number. The tradition that there were three comes from the three gifts.

[2] David N. Livingstone, *Darwin's Forgotten Defenders* (Grand Rapids: Eerdmans, 1987), p.xi. See also Ronald L. Numbers, *Creation by Natural Law: Laplace's Nebular Hypothesis in American Thought* (Seattle: University of Washington Press, 1977).

[3] Alexander Pope, "Essay on Man," About.com < http://classiclit.about.com/od/essayonmanapope/a/aa_essayonman_e1.htm>.

[4] Ronald L. Numbers, "Why Is Creationism So Popular in the USA?" The Faraday Institute of Science and Religion Multimedia, September 15, 2007 <www.st-edmunds.cam.ac.uk/faraday/Multimedia.php.>

[5] Livingstone, *Darwin's Forgotten Defenders.*

[6] Peter Bowler, *Evolution: History of an Idea* (Berkeley: University of California Press, 2003).

[7] Karl W. Giberson, "A Tale of Two Books," in *Saving Darwin: How to Be a Christian and Be-*

lieve in Evolution (New York: HarperOne, 2008), pp.43-63.

[8] Ibid., p.97.

[9] Ibid., p.98.

[10] Ibid., p.xi. See also Livingstone, *Darwin's Forgotten Defenders,* chap. 3.

[11] James McCosh of Princeton University is an example of the former, while Princeton Theological Seminary's Charles Hodge is an example of the latter. See Ronald L. Numbers, "Creationism History: Darwin Comes to America," Counterbalance Interactive Library <www.counterbalance.net/history/history-print.html>. See also Numbers, *Darwinism Comes to America* (Cambridge, Mass.: Harvard University Press, 1998).

[12] Warfield's views on the inerrancy of Scripture are quoted in the foreword by John C. McCampbell to John C. Whitcomb and Henry M. Morris, *The Genesis Flood: The Biblical Record and Its Scientific Implications* (Philadelphia: Presbyterian & Reformed, 1961), p.xx. His words were taken from Benjamin Breckinridge Warfield, "The Real Problem of Inspiration," in *The Inspiration and Authority of the Bible,* ed. Samuel G. Craig (Philadelphia: Presbyterian & Reformed, 1948).

[13] B. B. Warfield, quoted in Livingstone, *Darwin's Forgotten Defenders,* p.118.

[14] Numbers, *Darwinism Comes to America,* p.2.

[15] Benjamin Breckinridge Warfield, *Lectures on Anthropology* (Princeton, N.J.: Princeton University, 1888), quoted in Livingstone, *Darwin's Forgotten Defenders,* pp.118-19.

[16] Warfield believed that Moses was writing with his audience's education in mind: "Writing to meet the needs of men at large, [Moses] accommodated himself to their grade of intellectual preparation" (Benjamin Breckinridge Warfield, "Calvin's Doctrine of the Creation," *Princeton Theological Review* 13[1915]: 208-9, quoted in Livingstone, *Darwin's Forgotten Defenders,* p.120).

[17] Numbers, "Why Is Creationism So Popular?"

[18] Numbers, *Darwinism Comes to America,* p.4.

[19] Ronald L. Numbers, *The Creationists* (New York: A.A. Knopf, 1992), quoted in ibid.

[20] John C. Whitcomb and Henry M. Morris, *The Genesis Flood: The Biblical Record and Its Scientific Implications* (Philadelphia: Presbyterian & Reformed, 1961).

[21] Numbers, "Why Is Creationism So Popular?" See also Numbers, *Darwinism Comes to America,* pp.6-7.

[22] Michael Zeilik, *Astronomy: The Evolving Universe* (Cambridge: Cambridge University Press, 2002), p.153.

[23] Two examples of research groups working on the topic are Gerald Joyce at The Joyce Laboratory, Scripps Research Institute <www.scrip

ps.edu/mb/joyce> ; and Jack Szostak with the Origins of Life Initiative, Harvard University < www.harvardscience.harvard.edu/directory/pr ograms/origins-lifeinitiative> . Other recent publications on the subject include Robert M. Hazen, *Genesis: The Scientific Quest for Life's Origins* (Washington, D.C.: Joseph Henry Press, 2005); and Andrew H. Knoll, *Life on a Young Planet: The First Three Billion Years of Evolution on Earth* (Princeton, N.J.: Princeton University Press, 2003).

[24] It has been hypothesized that silicon may be an alternative to carbon, as it is structurally similar to carbon, with a half-filled outer shell and four free electrons, but as of yet it has not been shown to be a viable alternative because of differences in the way it reacts to other molecules. See, for example, Raymond Dessy, "Could Silicon Be the Basis for Alien Life Forms, Just as Carbon Is on Earth?" *Scientific American,* February 23, 1998 <www.scien tificameri can.com/article.cfm?id=0004212F-7 B73-1C72-9EB7809EC588F2D7>.

[25] Heinrich D. Holland, "Evidence for Life on Earth More Than 3850 Million Years Ago," *Science* 275, no.3 (1997):38-39.

[26] Charles Darwin, *The Life and Letters of Charles Darwin, Including an Autobiographical Chapter,* ed. Francis Darwin (London: John Murray, 1887), 3:18. See also Dr. John van Wyhe, ed.,

"The Complete Works of Charles Darwin Online," Darwin Online <http://darwin-online.org.uk/content/frameset?viewtype=text&itemID=F1452.3&pageseq=1>.

[27] See, e.g., Stephen Meyer, *The Signature in the Cell: DNA and the Evidence for Intelligent Design* (New York: HarperOne, 2009).

[28] Aleksandr I. Oparin, *The Origin of Life* (New York: Dover, 1952).

[29] Stanley L. Miller, "A Production of Amino Acids under Possible Primitive Earth Conditions," *Science* 117 (1953):528-29.

[30] Joan Oro, "Mechanism of Synthesis of Adenine from Hydrogen Cyanide under Possible Primitive Earth Conditions," *Nature* 191 (1961):1193-94.

[31] Michael P. Robertson and Stanley L. Miller, "An Efficient Prebiotic Synthesis of Cytosine and Uracil," *Nature* 375 (1995):772-24.

[32] W. Martin and M.J. Russell, "On the Origins of Cells: A Hypothesis for the Evolutionary Transitions from Abiotic Geochemistry to Chemoautotrophic Prokaryotes, and from Prokaryotes to Nucleated Cells," *Philosophical Transactions of the Royal Society: Biological Sciences* 358 (2003):59-85; and Jianghai Li and Timothy M. Kusky, "World's Largest Known Precambrian Fossil Black Smoker Chimneys and Associated Microbial Vent Communities, North China: Implications for Early Life," *Godwana Research* 12 (2007):84-100.

[33] Zachary Adam, "Actinides and Life's Origins," *Astrobiology* 7, no.6 (2007):852-72.

[34] Martin M. Hanczyc, Shelly M. Fujikawa and Jack W. Szostak, "Experimental Models of Primitive Cellular Compartments: Encapsulation, Growth, and Division," *Science* 302, no.5654 (2003):618-22.

[35] Francis Crick, *Life Itself: Its Origin and Nature* (New York: Simon & Schuster, 1981).

Chapter 7: What Is the Fine-Tuning of the Universe, and How Does It Serve as a Pointer to God?

[1] John Dervin, *From the Big Bang to the Big Brain* (West Conshohocken, Penn.: Infinity, 2003).

[2] The major exploration of this topic is John D. Barrow and Frank Tipler, *The Anthropic Cosmological Principle* (Oxford: Oxford University Press, 1986). For more about the different uses of the term *anthropic principle,* see John Polkinghorne, "The Anthropic Principle and the Science and Religion Debate," *Faraday Papers,* no.4 (2007) <www.st-edmunds.cam.ac.uk/faraday/resources/Faraday%20Papers/Faraday%20Paper%204%20Polkinghorne_EN.pdf>.

[3] Rodney D. Holder, "Is the Universe Designed?" *Faraday Papers,* no.10 (2007) <www.st-edmunds.cam.ac.uk/faraday/resources/Faraday%20Papers/Faraday%20Paper%2010%20Holder_EN.pdf>. See also John Polkinghorne, "The Science

and Religion Debate: An Introduction," *Faraday Papers,* no.1 (2007) <www.st-edmunds.cam.ac.uk/faraday/resources/Faraday%20Papers/F ara day%20Paper%201%20Polkinghorne_EN.pdf> ; and Francis S. Collins, *The Language of God: A Scientist Presents Evidence for Belief* (New York: Free Press, 2006).

[4] Since we don't understand how life formed and have experience only with carbon-based life, it is possible that self-replicating life forms might exist that are not based on carbon. We simply have no idea what form such life forms would take and whether they could evolve to any interesting stage of complexity. And there is absolutely no evidence of such alternative biochemistry. It seems unlikely that life could be based on any of the elements *lighter* than carbon, because they are too simple to generate complex proteins. And the atoms heavier than carbon are rarer (but no more complex). There is a compelling case that carbon is absolutely necessary for life.

[5] Fred Hoyle, "The Universe: Some Past and Present Reflections," *Engineering and Science* (1981):12, quoted in Holder, "Is the Universe Designed?"

[6] "Reference on Constants, Units, and Uncertainty: Proton-Electron Mass Ratio," National Institute of Standards and Technology Physics Labo-

ratory <http://physics.nist.gov/cgi-bin/cuu/Value?mpsme>.

[7] Holder, "Is the Universe Designed?"

[8] Alister McGrath, *A Finely-Tuned Universe: The Quest for God in Science and Theology* (Louisville: Westminster John Knox Press, 2009), p.176. For further reading about the biological fine-tuning of the environment, see specifically chaps. 10-11.

[9] Francis S. Collins, *The Language of God: A Scientist Presents Evidence for Belief* (New York: Free Press, 2006), pp.72-73. Specific numbers were taken from appendix A in John Polkinghorne and Nicholas Beale, *Questions of Truth* (Louisville: Westminster John Knox Press, 2009).

[10] John Leslie, *Universes* (London: Routledge, 1989), pp.13-14, quoted in Polkinghorne, "Science and Religion Debate."

[11] Alan Guth, *The Inflationary Universe* (Cambridge: Perseus Books, 1998).

[12] Holder, "Is the Universe Designed?" and Polkinghorne, "Science and Religion Debate."

[13] S. W. Hawking and Thomas Hertog, "Populating the Landscape: A Top Down Approach," arXiv.org, February 10, 2006 <http://arxiv.org/PS_cache/hep-th/pdf/0602/0602091v2.pdf>. Also in appendix A in Polkinghorne and Beale, *Questions of Truth.*

[14] Paul Davies, *Cosmic Jackpot: Why Our Universe Is Just Right for Life* (New York: Houghton Mifflin Harcourt, 2007), pp.151-90.

[15] Cornelius G. Hunter, *Darwin's Proof: The Triumph of Religion over Science* (Grand Rapids: Brazos, 2003), p.84.

[16] "Top Questions and Answers About Intelligent Design Theory," Center for Science and Culture, September 8, 2005 <www.discovery.org/a/2348>.

[17] Richard Milner and Vittorio Maestro, ed., "Intelligent Design?" *Natural History* (April 2002) < www.actionbioscience.org/evolution/nhmag.html>.

[18] Freeman Dyson, *Disturbing the Universe* (New York: Basic Books, 1979), p.250.

Chapter 8: Evolution and Human Beings

[1] Wim Kayzer, *A Glorious Accident* (New York: W.H. Freeman, 1997).

[2] These issues are explored in various ways in Thomas Jay Oord, ed., *Creation Made Free: Open Theology Engaging Science* (Eugene, Ore.: Pickwick, 2009), and Thomas Jay Oord, *Defining Love: A Philosophical, Scientific, and Theological Engagement* (Grand Rapids: Brazos, 2010), chap. 6.

[3] Stephen Jay Gould, *Wonderful Life: The Burgess Shale and the Nature of History* (New York: W.W. Norton, 1989), p.318.

[4] Ibid., p.289.

[5] Ibid., pp.141-45.

[6] Simon Conway Morris, "We Were Meant to Be..." *New Scientist* 176, no.2369 (2002):26.

[7] Simon Conway Morris, *Life's Solution: Inevitable Humans in a Lonely Universe* (New York: Cambridge University Press, 2003).

[8] Conway Morris, "We Were Meant to Be."

[9] Conway Morris, *Life's Solution,* p.xv.

[10] This spectrum of possible views is inspired by those presented in Denis Alexander, *Creation or Evolution: Do We Have to Choose?* (Oxford: Monarch Books, 2008).

[11] Jean Delumeau and Matthew O'Connell, *History of Paradise: The Garden of Eden in Myth and Tradition* (New York: Continuum, 1995).

[12] The genetic evidence is explained in Francis Collins, "Deciphering God's Instruction Book: The Lessons of the Human Genome," in *The Language of God* (New York: Free Press, 2006).

[13] Peter Enns, "Adam Is Israel," The BioLogos Forum, March 2, 2010 <http://biologos.org/blog/adam-is-israel>.

[14] See Alexander, *Creation or Evolution.*

[15] C.S. Lewis, *The Problem of Pain* (San Francisco: HarperSanFrancisco, 1996), pp.72-76.

[16] Karl Giberson, *Saving Darwin: How to Be a Christian and Believe in Evolution* (New York: HarperCollins, 2008), pp.13-15.

Invitation to Readers of This Book

The BioLogos Foundation invites you to join the conversation outlined in this book. Founded by Dr. Francis Collins in 2008, BioLogos has become the leading voice for evangelicals seeking harmony between science and faith. The Foundation is home to a growing group of Christians—professional scientists, biblical scholars, philosophers, theologians, pastors, educators and interested laypeople—concerned about the long history of conflict between the findings of science and ideas central to the Christian faith.

BioLogos affirms that the Bible is the inspired Word of God. We also believe that evolution, properly understood, best describes God's work of creation. We are committed to helping the church—and students, in particular—develop worldviews that embrace both of these complex belief structures, and that allow science and faith to co-exist peacefully.

If you are interested in joining the conversation or getting involved with us in any way, visit us at www.biologos.org. Or drop us a line at info@biologos.org.

Front Cover Flap

"Two challenging languages, one old and wise, one modern and awesome. Two very different accounts of human origins. Can the book of Scripture and the book of nature both be true in the age of science? We need sympathetic and enlightening interpreters. Happily Giberson and Collins here offer a guide to the perplexed that is reverent, relevant and very well-informed."

OWEN GINGERICH
Harvard-Smithsonian Center for Astrophysics, author of *God's Universe*

"Concise. Clear. Convincing. The Language of Science and Faith provides a straightforward means whereby the two sides of this contentious issue can get themselves on the same page. I recommend it as a resource for individuals and groups who want to believe that God speaks through both Scripture and nature."

DANIEL M. HARRELL
Ph.D., Colonial Church, Edina, Minnesota

"The theory of evolution raises important questions for Christians of all sorts, but this book is the best I've found to address the concerns of American evangelicals. It is written in clear enough language

to be accessible to students at a variety of levels, yet sophisticated enough to be of interest to professionals in both science and theology. It is at once intelligent and inspiring."

NANCEY MURPHY
Fuller Theological Seminary

"For too long, followers of Jesus have been told they have to make a choice—between science and Christianity, reason and belief, their intellectual integrity and their faith. The Language of Science and Faith is a readable and comprehensive resource for the thoughtful Christian who refuses to choose. Giberson and Collins tackle dif cult topics with charity, accessibility and integrity, moving the origins conversation forward in a way that honors God and builds up the church. This is a must-read for those who want to love the Lord with their heart, soul, mind and strength."

RACHEL HELD EVANS
Author of *Evolving in Monkey Town*

Back Cover Flap

"Collins and Giberson add a learned and engaging voice to the continuing struggle between Christian faith and scientific knowledge. The authors are central figures in advancing a true conversation between an ancient faith and modern ways of knowing, and it is hard to match their experience in dealing with the central questions covered in this volume. The Language of Science and Faith is an accessible distillation of their wisdom and I recommend it with great enthusiasm."

PETER ENNS
Senior Fellow in Biblical Studies,
The BioLogos Foundation

"As a pastor, I am constantly searching for resources that will guide people to the fullness of God. I care that my congregation be attracted toward God's artistry, moved by his majesty and intellectually challenged by his sovereignty. This book is at the top of my recommendations both as an evaluation of theories of creation and as a devotional that prompts us to revere the Creator."

DR. JOEL C. HUNTER
Northland Church, Longwood, Florida

KARL W. GIBERSON (Ph.D.) is an internationally known scholar who serves as professor of physics at Eastern Nazarene College, is the director of the Forum on Faith and Science at Gordon College, and is executive vice president of The BioLogos Foundation. Giberson has published over a hundred articles, reviews and essays and written five books, including *Saving Darwin.*

FRANCIS S. COLLINS (M.D., Ph.D.) is a world-renowned geneticist known for spearheading the Human Genome Project, which finished sequencing human DNA in 2003. He is director of the National Institutes of Health, founder of The BioLogos Foundation and author of the *New York Times* bestseller *The Language of God.*

Back Cover Material

IN THE BEGINNING GOD CREATED THE HEAVENS AND THE EARTH. Genesis 1:1

Christians affirm that everything exists because of God—from subatomic quarks to black holes. Science often claims to explain nature without including God in the picture at all. Which do we choose?

The good news is that we do not have to decide. Science does not overthrow the Bible. Faith does not require rejecting science. World-renowned geneticist Francis Collins, author of *The Language of God,* along with fellow scientist Karl Giberson show how we can embrace both. Their fascinating treatment explains how God cares for and interacts with his creation while science offers a reliable way to understand the world he made.

Together they clearly answer dozens of the most common questions people ask about Darwin, evolution, the age of the earth, the Bible, the existence of God and our finely tuned universe.

The authors disentangle the false conclusions of Christians and atheists alike about science and evolution from the actual results of research in astronomy, physics, geology and genetics. In its place they find a story of the grandeur and beauty of a world made by a supremely creative God.

"This book is destined to become a classic for those who, with an open mind, are willing to seriously

wrestle with questions about the relationship of modern science with Christian faith. It is not for the faint of heart but is a treasure trove for those willing to dig deep into this critical subject."

DR. TIM JOHNSON
Senior medical contributor for ABC News
and author of *Finding God in the Questions*

A

B

C

H

I

J

K

L

M

N

O

P

Q

R

S

T

Y

Books For ALL Kinds of Readers

At ReadHowYouWant we understand that one size does not fit all types of readers. Our innovative, patent pending technology allows us to design new formats to make reading easier and more enjoyable for you. This helps improve your speed of reading and your comprehension. Our EasyRead printed books have been optimized to improve word recognition, ease eye tracking by adjusting word and line spacing as well as minimizing hyphenation. Our EasyRead SuperLarge editions have been developed to make reading easier and more accessible for vision-impaired readers. We offer Braille and DAISY formats of our books and all popular E-Book formats.

Made in the USA
Las Vegas, NV
24 December 2020